THE NEW PROFESSIONAL SALESPERSON

Meeting Challenges in the 21st Century

THE NEW PROFESSIONAL SALESPERSON

Meeting Challenges in the 21st Century

WALTER VIEIRA

ATLANTIC

PUBLISHERS & DISTRIBUTORS (P) LTD

ATLANTIC
PUBLISHERS & DISTRIBUTORS (P) LTD
7/22, Ansari Road, Darya Ganj, New Delhi
Tel.: +91-11-4077 5252, 2327 3880
E-mail: orders@atlanticbooks.com
Web: www.atlanticbooks.com

Published by Atlantic Publishers & Distributors (P) Ltd 2024

Previously Published by SAGE Publications in 2008

Printed & bound in India by Atlantic Print Services

For Philip Kotler
a friend, guide, mentor
'always a willing, helping hand'
for two decades

Contents

Foreword by Rolph Anderson ix
Preface xi
Acknowledgements xiii

1. Selling of Ideas 1
2. A Series of Challenges 9
3. A Theory and Structure in Selling 24
4. Planning for the Sale 39
5. Self-Management in Selling 50
6. Focussing on the Customer 61
7. Making the Sales Presentation 75
8. Objections—When the Customer Says 'No' 90
9. The Close and Thereafter 103
10. Compulsions and Reflections 108
11. Selling in the 21st Century 141

Index 150
About the Author 153

Foreword

Professional personal selling is undergoing a dramatic change worldwide as we go through the 21st century. New ways are being explored to provide greater value-added services and develop mutually profitable, ongoing relationships with customers. Several technological, behavioural and managerial forces are inexorably influencing buyer–seller relationships, and dramatically changing how sales activities are carried out.

To succeed in the new century, salespeople will need to learn new roles and reinvent some old ones, such as learning more about their customers' businesses and taking responsibility for customer profitability; helping customers create long-term competitive advantages; learning how to use their company resources to create added value for customers; building good relationships with their own headquarters' support team; devoting more attention to intelligence gathering as the 'eyes and ears' of their companies in the marketplace; making use of the latest technology to increase customer contact and service while reducing costs; and establishing long-term, mutually profitable partnerships with customers.

But, beyond all these new and revised roles, salespeople will still need old-fashioned personal pride and individual style to be successful.

Walter Vieira, an internationally respected sales and marketing consultant, frequent lecturer at major universities, and prolific author of books and articles, shows in his witty, inimitable and anecdotal way that professional pride will always be an essential ingredient for salespeople in gaining the respect and interest of the customer for successful negotiations.

The New Professional Salesperson provides special sales insights and actionable advice that can be translated into greater professional personal selling success in the 21st century.

Rolph Anderson
Royal H. Gibson, Sr Chair Professor of Marketing
Drexel University
Philadelphia, Pennsylvania, USA

Preface

There are so many books on selling that are available all over the world. Why another book on the same subject? Has enough not been said already? The answer is difficult—because it is both yes and no.

I have read many books on selling. Most of them are very long and specialised, occupying a 'niche', such as *Sales Cybernetics* by Brian Adams and *Psycho Sales Analysis* by Jack Huttig. Most of them belabour the application of theory to practice, while others only tell stories of sales successes and failures without any reference to theory.

I have interacted with thousands of salespersons in a career spanning 45 years—as a salesperson, sales executive, marketing manager and management consultant; as a recruiter and trainer of sales personnel; and as a visiting professor at business schools. I have worked with sales personnel in the US, UK, Middle East, Africa, South Asia and South East Asia. I have found that most salespersons are action oriented, impatient, inclined to be mobile, up and about rather than sitting and thinking; friendly and outgoing; and ready to see the bright side of life and laugh. They have no inclination to sit aside quietly and read a tome—however useful this may be professionally. Of course, they should. But most don't!

Hence this book—the distillate of all that I have read, seen and observed over 45 years. A fusion of theory and good practices in selling. A record of observations as stories from a raconteur's bag of anecdotes. Sales jokes—some obvious, some tongue-in-cheek—which will provide relief with a good laugh. 'Questions to Reflect On' and 'Action Points' at the end of each chapter that will make salespersons think and tempt them to read other books to find the answers. Or they can use these as starting points for discussion in sales meetings to hone their skills through interaction with peers.

A book which they will be inclined to glance through or preferably read, and keep in the bag as part of the sales kit—to read, revise and amuse themselves during the innumerable waiting periods in customers' office anterooms.

All this effort is a contribution towards the development of the profession of selling and the evolution of the professional salesperson for the 21st century!

Acknowledgements

I am grateful to Rolph Anderson for writing the 'Foreword'. I have been greatly impressed by his works, particularly *Professional Personal Selling,* which I feel is the most comprehensive and complete book on selling.

And my gratitude to the thousands of salespersons I have met and worked with, across three continents, over 40 years—who have taught me all I know and which I have distilled in this book, so that many other thousands may benefit.

Special thanks to my secretary, Philomena Fonseca, who has spent time and effort in typing the manuscript, which has undergone modifi cations so many times.

CHAPTER 1

Selling of Ideas

SELLING—AN OLD AND DEMANDING PROFESSION

Selling is not a new profession. In fact, it may be considered to be the world's oldest profession. In the Bible, in the very first stories depicting Adam and Eve, we are told of the serpent (the evil one) who *sold* an idea to Eve—the idea of eating the forbidden fruit. Eve *bought* the idea, and even *sold* it to Adam. Having eaten the fruit, Adam and Eve were cast out of Paradise (the Garden of Eden) by God for disobeying his orders.

This does not imply that selling is wrong. It only shows that selling is as old as mankind itself.

There has always been an exchange of goods, services or ideas, for some value—whether cash or kind or any other form. Perhaps the person who sold these goods, services or ideas was not labelled a 'salesperson' nor was the process called 'selling'. But the essence of selling remains the same, irrespective of terminology and modern or sophisticated labels.

On a Lighter Note

The head of a large organisation handed out cigars to everybody one morning. 'My son made his first Rs 300 yesterday since he got out of college a year ago. He sold the watch we gave him for graduation.'

WELCOME TO THE CLUB

This welcome is adapted from an address to new teachers in New York by Principal S. Robert Shapiro. I found this to be a brief, yet complete and very appropriate basis for all that I have to say in the pages that follow:

> As I welcome you to our company I should like to assume a magician's role and present to you five magic gifts—gifts of the mind and spirit, far more valuable than tangible worldly goods.
>
> First, I give you *enthusiasm* that continues undiminished through the years, so that you may remain forever young in mind and spirit.
>
> Second, I give you *happiness in your work*—the thrill of experimenting with new methods and techniques, the satisfaction that comes with the consummation of worthwhile endeavours, and the wholehearted joy that will fill your being as you watch your sales and customers grow.
>
> Third, I give you a *love for customers*; for without such love, the selling task can be a burden.
>
> Fourth, I give you a *truly professional attitude*, the desire to improve on your own, the will to make yourself a better person, the spirit of cooperation with colleagues, superiors and competitors, and the insight as well as the desire to see and support the best in your colleagues and superiors.
>
> And fifth, I give you a *yearning for ideals* and the *courage to meet the many setbacks* you may suffer while working to attain your ideals.
>
> May you have the practical sense to realise that our ideals are distant, and we attain only milestones on the road to our ultimate goals. The thrill in selling is in the striving for the ideal.

WE ARE ALL SALESPERSON

The label 'salesperson' is applied to those who earn their living by selling a product or a service. However, this is a very narrow definition because in a way we all are salespersons. We need to be good salespersons in order to make a success of any profession.

A doctor needs to have more than just a knowledge of medicine. He needs to inspire confidence in the patient with his warmth and friendliness. He has to sell himself. A lawyer has to put forth his arguments coherently and convincingly. He is selling himself and his ideas.

Company chairmen have to convince shareholders, inspire confidence in them and carry them along. In some primitive societies, bachelors had to kill a jaguar, in order to prove their skill at hunting, to inspire confidence in the bride's family and win a bride.

Whether it is a child wanting a toy, a balloon or a lollipop, or a politician campaigning with his election promises to a generally sceptical audience of voters—they are all selling, although they may not be called salesperson!

> *On a Lighter Note*
>
> A good salesperson is one who can convince his wife that its a shame to hide such a beautiful figure under a full length mink coat.

SELLING EVOLUTION IN COUNTRIES

In the least developed countries, you will generally see selling of products. As countries evolve into developing or developed countries, you will see a greater number of services being sold.

In highly developed countries, you will find that in addition to the selling of services, there is also a lot of selling of ideas. Thus the number of patents and copyrights registered are the highest in the highly developed countries, and these are sold to the developing or less developed countries.

> *It is not so important to know everything*
> *as to know the exact value of everything,*
> *to appreciate what we learn,*
> *and to arrange what we know.*
>
> —H. Moore

SATISFYING CUSTOMER NEEDS

It is said that in some parts of the world, the word 'salesperson' is used derogatorily. Some go further in describing 'a great salesperson' as one who can sell refrigerators to an Eskimo or hair oil to a bald man. Such remarks only denigrate the profession of selling.

A good salesperson fulfils either a present or future need of the customer. He does not just sell. He makes the customer want to buy. A good doctor does not give medicines to a healthy person. However, he may prescribe a preventive. Similarly, a salesperson not only sells to meet a present need, but also sells to a potential customer who may have a need in the future and does not require the product or service right now.

This is why a good salesperson is a problem solver. He solves the customer's problem and in the process sells his product. Occasionally, he may even solve the customer's problem without recommending his own product because another product, perhaps a competitor's, meets the customer's need more appropriately. That is why salespersons need to keep asking themselves everyday—am I really selling or am I just taking orders? Do I really help people or am I hustling them?

A CRITICAL ROLE IN THE ECONOMY

We often do not realise that in a large measure the wheels of economies have been kept in motion by salespersons. They have been playing a pivotal role in 'improving the standard of living', both in developing and developed countries.

American Investment Banker Paul Mazur has defined marketing in its simplest form—as 'the delivery of a standard of living'. The final interface in this process is between the salesperson and the customer.

All the technical research, production techniques, financial management and personnel specialisation would come to naught, if salespersons did not tread new geographical areas, make people aware, get them to appreciate the benefits and make them want to buy, so that they can lead better, more fulfilling and satisfied lives.

There are situations where sales skills is misused to cheat people or to create undesirable wants. But then, any profession can be misused to wrong ends, whether medicine, law, engineering or any other.

On a Lighter Note

Fr. Joe admonishing his flock on the evils of business ended his sermon with: 'And remember brothers and sisters, there will be no buying and selling in heaven.' A salesperson in the back row grumbled: 'That's not where business has gone, anyway.'

An individual has not started
living until he can rise
above the narrow confines
of his individualistic concerns
to the broader concerns of all humanity.

—Martin Luther King Jr

ROLE IN THE EVOLUTION OF SOCIETY

In many ways, it is the salesperson who has played a key role in the evolution of human society, right from the barter stage to the age of money exchange, from the age of cavemen and small agro communities to the Industrial Revolution, and now to the age of marketing.

The barter stage, where one sold to another, with an exchange of goods or services of approximate equivalent value, had its problems, with one having a cow to sell but only a pair of slippers to buy. So people moved to the age of money exchange.

With the invention of the steam engine and the advent of the Industrial Revolution, salespersons were called to play a critical and important role. They had to urgently expand markets and match the demand to the greatly increased production.

In the present age of marketing, the proliferation of identical products and the emergence of the discriminating customer have made it necessary to first find out what the customer wants, and then design, produce and sell the product to him at the right price, in the right place and at the right time. That is why the definition of marketing by Paul Mazur, as 'the delivery of a standard of living', is so acceptable from a salesperson's viewpoint.

Marketing is an art and a science, of which product planning, pricing, distribution and promotion, advertising and selling are integral parts. This is called the marketing mix.

A man can't make a place
for himself in the sun,
if he keeps taking refuge
under the family tree.

—Helen Keller

A DEMANDING PROFESSION

Selling is a very demanding profession. Contrary to popular opinion, everyone is not suited or cut out for selling. And selling is certainly not for those who amble into it, thinking it is an easy way to make quick money, or to take jaunts around the country, or make a large circle of acquaintances, or have an opportunity to 'dress in style'.

Selling requires hard work without fixed hours, and adjusting to timings when the customer will be available. It requires continuous learning because the environment is always changing. The customer profile, attitudes and habits change, so do competitors and competitive strategies; new technologies and, therefore, new products continuously throw the most carefully laid out plans out of gear.

The price of greatness is responsibility.

—Winston Churchill

THE FREEDOM TO BE, OR NOT TO BE

It is a strange contradiction that the more freedom you have, the greater is the responsibility that you do not misuse this freedom. This is why a democracy expects greater responsibility from its citizens, who are expected to behave in a responsible manner, follow certain rules, some written and some unwritten, and to look at the general good of the community rather than their own selfish interests or convenience.

In a democracy, a citizen 'may or may not', unlike 'must or must not' in a dictatorship. And because he 'may or may not', he has to think about the consequences of every action, to see whether it will benefit him to the detriment of some others or everyone else, or whether it will benefit him as well as the others.

The salesperson in a corporation is in a similar situation. He is unlike the employee in works, accounts, administration, personnel or purchase, who has to clock in at a certain hour and who cannot clock out before a certain hour. He is not watched and will not be noticed in case of absence for any reasonable period of time. The salesperson works in a 'boundary-less time zone'. No one can really know when he starts his day, whether at seven or ten in the morning, or when he ends his day, whether at five or nine in the evening. Or what breaks he takes in between, and for how long.

The salesperson is on his own, with more or less complete freedom. He can spend the time making calls, or be at the movie house or coffee shop. No one will really know. The sales figures at the end of the month might give an indication. But sometimes even these can be misleading. Sales may grow in spite of the salesperson, and they may fall in spite of his efforts and devotion.

Like a citizen in a democracy, a salesperson is in charge of his own destiny. He can be just as good as he wants to be. He can be disciplined and have the courage and good sense to impose this discipline on himself. He can be lax and careless and think that he is taking the company for a ride. Only he can decide for himself. And he will decide right only when he realises and never forgets that with the freedom that comes with his job, also comes the responsibility for doing it well, honestly and to the best of his ability.

On a Lighter Note

'How many salespersons work for you?' I asked. The sales manager replied, 'Just about half.'

QUESTIONS TO REFLECT ON

1. Can you identify some professions where selling is not needed? Which are these? And why is selling not needed?
2. Can you think of any three real life examples where a salesperson has solved a customer's problem without recommending his own product?
3. Can you think of two other definitions of 'marketing' apart from Paul Mazur's?
4. Can you identify five products or services where salespersons have to work before or after 'accepted' work hours?
5. What are the 'indicators' that a salesperson has no pride in his profession?
6. Why do clients hesitate to pay for ideas?
7. Ca n you add to Principal Shapiro's five magic gifts?

8. Can you identify two identical products wherein selling has made the difference to one of them?

ACTION POINTS

> I suggest that you actually write down the Answers to the Action Points at the end of each Chapter. This will help to make the subject clearer to you, and enable to you do an effective self-analysis.

1. Why did I become a salesperson?
2. What other job would I prefer to do? Why?
3. What are the advantages/disadvantages of my present job?
4. What does my family think about my job?
5. What do my friends think about my job?
6. What do I contribute to society through my work?
7. What more can I do to increase my contribution?
8. Am I learning all the time:
   - about my customers?
   - about my competition?
   - about my products?
9. From whom am I learning:
   - through books?
   - from my boss?
   - from my peers?
   - from training programmes?
   - from my competitors?
   - from my customers?
10. Do my customers respect me because they think I have mastery of my subject?
11. What can I do to make my company proud of me?
12. What can I do to improve the image of sales skills:
    - among my juniors?
    - among colleagues in the profession?
    - within the company?
    - within the community and society?

Chapter 2

A Series of Challenges

Today is the greatest day I ever lived,
and tomorrow is going to be better!

—Anonymous

Selling requires a positive attitude towards challenges. A customer is never won over permanently. An order obtained on one occasion does not translate into a customer for life.

Between one interview and the next, the profile of the customer has changed. He has met with the competitor's salesperson, he has been reading newspapers and technical journals, and he has met others in the industry and exchanged notes. The customer is not the same person the salesperson had met a fortnight or three months ago. In psychographic terms, he has changed, although physically he may appear to be the same person. Therefore, every interview is a new challenge. A salesperson facing a customer has to virtually start all over again, every time, without taking anything or anyone for granted.

On a Lighter Note

The sales manager was telling Jude the new salesperson, that the former salesperson he was replacing had messed up the territory so much, that he, the replacement, will experience a most difficult time getting any order out of the chaos.

Jude reassured the sales manager: 'I don't know who this fellow Chaos is, but I'll get an order from him, even if I have to call on him every day of the year.'

NEW TRENDS AFFECTING PERSONAL SELLING

'Change is inevitable in every field, but eight mega trends make personal selling one of today's most volatile careers,' says Rolph Anderson in his book *Professional Personal Selling*. These worldwide trends are:

- Buyers are more aware and demanding.
- Customer expectations are rising.
- Revolutionary advances in telecommunications and computer technology are happening all the time.
- Sales force for consumer products is shrinking.
- Women and minorities are flooding the sales profession.
- Domestic markets are undergoing micro-segmentation.
- Foreign competition is intensifying.
- Markets are being internationalised.

A wise salesperson will keep these trends in mind while going about his work.

Sales Don't Just Happen

80 per cent of all sales are made after the fifth call.

48 per cent of all salespersons call once, and quit.

25 per cent call twice, and quit.

10 per cent keep on calling.

These 10 per cent make 80 per cent of the sales.

SUCCESS CAN CAUSE FAILURE

Prof. Philip Kotler, professor of marketing at Kellogg Business School, NW University, US, an eminent authority on marketing, has said that 'many times, as corporations grow larger, they begin to forget the very lessons which have made them a success.'

Look around the country. There were large agency houses, which were citadels of market power only 50 years ago. These were strong selling organisations that imported goods and then distributed and promoted them successfully—from *Tootal* ties to *Horlicks* and *Brylcreem*. But where are these now? Some products and companies have disappeared, or have completely transformed. And there are reasons why this happens. It is a list of failures at many levels of the company, right from the chief executive to the salesperson:

1. When the *number of levels in the hierarchy increases*, it becomes difficult for the ultimate consumer to have his voice heard at the topmost levels, where it matters most.
2. When it does get heard, the *communication is so distorted* that what is finally heard is completely different from what was originally said.
3. The levels close to the decision makers at the top keep *feeding information that will be liked*, rather than what is true.
4. The *salesperson become over confident* because the product is popular and sells. They make fewer calls, with less travel. They think of their own convenience rather than the requirements of the customer.
5. The salesperson begin to *take the customer for granted*. It's a take it or leave it attitude. They know that the customer cannot leave it.
6. The salesperson and the company may try to *twist the customer's arm*, tying up slow moving products to fast moving ones and forcing the customer to buy, however reluctantly.
7. The *salesperson become insensitive and unobservant* about the competition. This invariably ends up as the 'tortoise and hare' story. The hare realises he has lost the race, but only too late to correct the situation.
8. The salesperson *rely on 'improvising'* rather than on the system and planning. Again—a sign of over confidence and 'cockiness'.

Yes, many companies fail, because they forget the very lessons they had learnt and used to become successful!

Failure is instructive
The person who really thinks
Learns quite as much from his failures,
As from his successes.

—John Dewey

SUCCESS CAN BREED SUCCESS

It may be true that failure is the stepping stone to success. Most times, for most people, it is. And some of the time, this adage is true for salesperson as well. But it needs a modification. The salesperson works under strange and unusual conditions. All the time, people around him are eroding his morale and his sense of self-worth. They may not be doing this on purpose. It just turns out that way.

The dealer complains that the consignments are greatly delayed, or that the damages are high and the packaging needs improvement. The customer complains about high prices or performance below expectations. The branch office complains that the salesperson is spending too much time in the office rather than in the field. The wife complains that he is spending too much time out of the headquarters on tour. Surrounded by such antipathy, unconscious though it may be, the salesperson's morale is under attack all the time.

Therefore, he has to build his own defences. And these are strongly built, only with the bricks and stones of success. Success boosts his morale to withstand all attacks. He knows that irrespective of what people around him say (or sometimes do), he goes on from strength to strength. Sales keep coming in. Profits keep increasing. Sales commissions keep growing. And he keeps his head high, while his confidence levels are even higher.

From his personal selling success, he develops an inner strength, a 'steel inside' as it were, of self-confidence, which no one, not even his bitterest of critics, can damage or destroy. He knows he is always on top of the situation. He knows he will always win, in the long run, as he has in the past.

Success in selling comes from many factors, all centred around knowledge of the product, of the customer, of the market, and the ability to communicate and close. Most salesperson capitalise on their strengths in some of these areas. Only some salespersons will have equal strengths in all areas. But the important thing is to have more successes than failures—to increase the 'hit rate' as they would say in baseball.

A high hit rate and, therefore, a high success attitude will distinguish the great salespersons from the also-rans. The latter will be consigned to the group of those who get out every morning to meet people who don't want to see them, to talk to people who don't want to listen to them, to sell to people who don't want to buy from them. They make calls. They don't make sales. They are travellers, not salesperson. They assume failure even before they have failed. And one failure then follows another, rather than one success following another!

> *We know what we are,*
> *but know not what we may be.*
>
> —William Shakespeare

THE SALESPERSON NEEDS 'INNER STRENGTH'

Selling demands product knowledge, market knowledge, knowledge of customer psychology, innovative thinking, physical stamina for extensive travel and an alert mind.

But most of all, it demands 'inner strength' from the salesperson—the ability to not get depressed at the end of each day after he has done his rounds, having gone to see people who may not have wanted to see him, talked to people who may not have wanted to listen to him, tried to sell to people who may not have wanted to buy from him.

The salesperson needs inner strength to learn from every interview and from the mistakes he has made, and then to change his strategy accordingly. He needs it to make sure that he does not let a single interview ruin the rest of the day's work. He needs it to make his last interview of the day as good and as fresh as the first.

On a Lighter Note

Colonel: Soldier what was your occupation before being drafted?
Soldier: Salesperson.
Colonel: Good, you'll get plenty of orders here.

******

Salesperson: Are you sure the boss is not in his office?
Secretary: Do you doubt his word?

THE EVER-CHANGING PROFESSION

Arthur Miller's *Death of a Salesperson* was a contribution not only to literature, but also to the body of knowledge on salespersonship. It is a touching story of a salesperson, Billy Lohman, who did not change his attitude and style to suit the changing environment. Once successful, he was finally asked to go, because over a period of two decades, he refused to see change and, therefore, did not change himself.

Billy tried to sell to customers by telling jokes, by entertaining them over drinks and dinner, by giving small gifts. But times had changed. The customer now wanted product knowledge, competitive advantage, product benefits and high returns on investment. Billy was at sea in this new environment. He tried pushing through with old methods and he failed miserably.

The salesperson is not dead—he has changed. The old style of selling is dead, but a new type has emerged. As long as humanity exists, salespersonship will exist—selling of goods, services or ideas will never become an obsolete function.

However, salespersonship will have to be continuously updated, just as in any other profession, to keep up with new knowledge, new ideas and a new environment.

On a Lighter Note

When you realise how little inefficient salesperson produce, you wonder what they will do when they retire, or are they already retired and don't know it?

******

It has been said that some inept salesperson die at the age of 30, but remain on the payroll and are not buried until they reach the age of 60!

Knowledge itself is power.

—Francis Bacon

WHO IS A PROFESSIONAL?

Many people have misunderstandings about the selling assignment. They do not look upon it as a career. It is something that one does, until one finds something else, something better to do. It is a period of incubation until one becomes either a sales executive or moves into a sales planning function. Therefore, the question repeatedly asked is: 'Is selling a profession?'

An unusual and well-produced film called *The Professional* tries to provide an answer. The main role of the salesperson is played by Van Johnson, a famous Hollywood actor of yesteryears. This film puts forward the theory that selling is a profession, just like any other profession—medicine, engineering or architecture.

The film sets down five criteria for the professional salesperson:

1. He must have the *will to learn,* and keep on learning throughout his professional career. He needs to update his knowledge, skills and techniques every year, irrespective of how many years he may have worked in the field.
2. He must serve a period of *internship,* to learn the ropes and the details from someone senior and more experienced, just as a surgeon learns from a senior surgeon by assisting at operations.
3. He must *specialise* because, even in selling, there is need to have expertise in specific products or services. The knowledge required in selling hotel services is different from the knowledge required in selling switchgears. Though the basic lessons of selling may remain the same, the details will differ considerably.
4. He must take time to *fraternise,* to meet others in the same profession and exchange ideas and opinions, and measure himself against his peers.
5. He must have the desire to *contribute*—to the community, to society, to the country. Selling is not just a selfish job. It is a profession which goes beyond oneself and stretches on to a wider canvas.

Therefore, selling is a profession. It should be seen, perceived and projected as one, by a community of salesperson who act professionally.

You can stand tall
without standing on someone.
You can be a victor
without having victims.

—Harriet Woods

HE WHO GIVES DOES NOT BECOME POORER

Joe Rodrigues was the medical representative for an American pharmaceutical company, Pfizer, with headquarters in Jabalpur. When I first started selling, I was posted to this town and met him on my first working day in the field. 'Are you new here?' he asked. I replied that I was, and he asked me whether I was new to the profession also. When I said yes again, he offered to work with me for two days and introduce me to the leading doctors and chemists. I readily agreed.

We had competitive products. An antibiotic price war was on, in which our two companies played the leading roles. Yet, Joe took me around. He introduced me, encouraged me and gave me confidence. He even helped with my detailing to doctors, and asked chemists for orders on my behalf. After two days, he said, 'Now Walter, I have done my part. We can now fight in the marketplace.'

Later I discovered that Joe's product knowledge was so good and up-to-date that he was invited by the Medical Association every year to give a lecture on some aspect of the latest developments in medicine. Joe was a science undergraduate. The regular invitation was a credit to his level of knowledge.

Joe taught me what a truly professional salesperson should be. And he taught me that 'you never stoop, when you stoop to help a child.'

FROM OCCUPATION TO PROFESSION

An occupation becomes a profession when it meets the following four criteria:

1. A *body of technical knowledge*, which has been collected and collated over many years.
   As it meets this criterion, selling is a profession.
2. A *system of examinations* for entry and periodic updating of required knowledge.
   The selling profession is yet to adopt this fully.
3. There is a *commitment to serve the customer* with a controlled use of knowledge.
   Most outstanding salesperson would not be outstanding if they did not put the customer first.

4. A *code of ethics*, which is followed for self-policing by the professionals.
   There is an unwritten code that the salesperson will not make false claims for his product and that he will make full disclosures, etc. But this has not been formalised as a written code in most companies.

Perhaps if an association of salesperson were to be formed as a truly national professional body, adopting all these four criteria, selling can be brought from the level of an occupation to that of a profession. The salesperson would then have pride and style when he enters the profession; he would look upon it as a career rather than a stepping stone to being a sales executive, and would also retire from the profession with his head held high, rather than as a failure who 'never made it'.

There are privately-sponsored sales associations and privately-run selling programmes which do not have the same accreditation as professional bodies like the Institute of Chartered Accountants, the Institute of Engineers or the Institute of Management Consultants. However, the starting of private programmes is a good beginning from which the professional national body will eventually evolve.

Managements also have a role to play in elevating selling to a profession. 'What are you doing here in the office?' is a question asked when the salesperson comes to the head office with an occasional problem. This attitude needs to change.

The other is with regard to remuneration. The salesperson should be allowed to earn on the basis of his productivity. If his performance is excellent, his rewards should also be excellent. Since his performance is measurable, there is no problem of vagueness on this score. The top-ranking salesperson with many years of experience could perhaps earn as much as, or more than, a younger sales executive, and there would be nothing wrong with that. If this attitude could pervade organisations, then many salesperson who hanker to be promoted (but are unsuited for a managerial position) would continue to do what they like to do, to excel in it and be rewarded well for it. The managerial job would hold no attraction for the career salesperson just because of the higher remuneration.

In a large pharmaceutical company, the sales director was surprised when one of the senior salesperson who was promoted to sales supervisor refused the promotion and, with a sense of drama, tore the promotion letter publicly in the presence of his colleagues. His argument was that the emoluments would be about the same as he was getting now, but as a salesperson he was 'protected' by union regulations and he would lose this protection as a sales supervisor.

How much nicer it would be if the same decision could have been arrived at, without the touch of drama, and not for the reasons he gave, but because he prefers to sell and enjoys it. He is well rewarded for it and does not want to be a sales supervisor.

Selling as a career and as a profession would then have arrived in India. Top 'salesperson clubs' would have started out, like in the US. There would be style and pride in the profession, and salesperson would not be referred to as 'agents' any more, because customers and the general public would notice a change in their conduct, bearing, operations and, most important, in the way they look at themselves.

The few among them who have the aptitude, the attributes and the potential to be successful managers, to get work done through other people, would move on. Many among them are essentially loners and like to be independent and self-motivated, but are incapable of motivating other members of a team, coordinating their work or controlling it. And they will continue to carry the salesperson's bag till the retirement day, and not be ashamed of it. In fact, they will be proud of it!

AN UNWRITTEN CODE AMONG PROFESSIONALS

We have often been impressed by the way banana vendors follow an unwritten code.

Ram comes early at seven in the morning, shouting to make his presence felt. The bananas are getting black and ripe, perhaps overripe, and are priced at just Rs 6 a dozen. The housewives are already alert. They come out to their balconies and place their orders.

An hour later, another vendor comes down the road. The bananas are just right. Not too ripe. And they are Rs 6.50 a dozen. A little later, another vendor comes down, with even fresher and better bananas, priced at Rs 8 a dozen. But most housewives have already bought bananas earlier. They look down, with a tinge of regret. The banana vendor is also sorry, but he is not as regretful. Those who stand to lose more are given priority, as per the code of honour among salesperson. Today it is Ram's turn, tomorrow it could be someone else. No man is an island unto himself, especially in selling!

THE LONG-TERM VISION FOR LONG-TERM SALES

I was a management trainee in 1961, working for Glaxo in Mumbai. One of my stints was as an executive assistant to the sales director. I sat outside his cabin, at a small table, in the first row down the corridor, in a large open hall.

There were many advertising managers who came in to see the sales director. They met his secretary, sent in their visiting cards and were ushered in. When they finished, they went away, either with a contract for advertisements in their journal, or several times, without one.

But there was one in this group who represented the well-known magazine *Reader's Digest*. He was not an overpowering personality. Short, pleasant and always neatly dressed, he went about his business quietly and unobtrusively, but effectively. He had all his figures—the profile of the readers of his magazine, the kind of products and services which would benefit most from advertising in it, the cost of reach for each contact, etc.

And every time he came out of the boss' cabin, he stopped at my table to sit there for a little while, exchange a few pleasantries and move on. In my marketing career, he was the first person to give me a profile of his magazine and also the first to send me a complimentary copy of his monthly. I was impressed by his kindness in spending time with a mere management trainee.

Many years later, I was the marketing chief of my company, and this advertising manager had become a director in his. I never forgot the thoughtfulness and kindness he had shown years earlier. His representatives were always welcome to see me, and his journal always featured in my ad schedule justifiably, but also with a touch of nostalgia and gratitude.

A PROFESSION WITH A DIFFERENCE

As mentioned earlier, there are four criteria which a profession must have, in order to be labelled a 'profession'. Selling meets most of these criteria to a large extent and can be called a profession just like any other.

Selling is a profession where *no minimum formal qualifications* are required for entry. In course of time, such qualifications may be insisted upon by employers. Employers today may insist on graduation, or an engineering degree, or any other qualification or technical skills that will facilitate the selling of the product. However, it is not a diploma or degree in selling that they are asking for. This is an advantage to new entrants.

There is *no age barrier* to enter and exit the selling profession. One can begin selling at the age of 16 and quit at 30, or one can start at 45 and quit at 65. Such flexibility does not exist in most other professions. It is unlikely that you will be admitted into a medical college at 35 or start a successful legal practice at 45. It can happen but it is rare.

In selling, you are *not dependent on accoutrements*. A surgeon cannot operate without instruments, or an engineer without a slide rule and other paraphernalia. But selling depends only on the use of the human mind. It is one mind influencing another. All the rest, such as visual aids and demonstration kits, are only aids. They are not essential to the process of selling. And this gives the selling profession flexibility.

Selling is a profession where *mistakes are easily remedied*. One bad interview need not affect subsequent interviews. Failure with one customer need not cast a shadow over all other customers. Every mistake is containable. Therefore, given the attitude and the will, success in selling is easier. These are all advantages in the profession of selling. Salesperson should use these to their own advantage, to make progress.

THE AMBASSADOR OF HIS COMPANY

It has been said that a salesperson is an ambassador of his company. After all, the customer will perhaps never meet the chairman of the board of directors. It is unlikely that he will meet the managing director. There is a small chance that he may meet the marketing director. Once in a while he may meet the marketing manager, and perhaps once every year the sales manager.

But the only person the customer will meet on a regular basis is the salesperson who looks after the specific territory and who services the customer every fortnight, or every month, or every two months, or whatever the frequency of visits is for that particular industry and company.

The customer forms his impression of the company and its products, largely based on his impression of the salesperson. If the salesperson is well groomed and neatly dressed, proper in behaviour and speech, not too loud or aggressive, and if his kit is well maintained externally and well organised within, the customer is bound to conclude that the company and its products are similarly of a high quality. The salesperson, therefore, projects an image of the company like an ambassador does for his country.

The salesperson is a *link* between the company and the customer. The salesperson thus *communicates* with the customer on behalf of the company, providing information, clarifications, reasons for purchase, benefits obtained, price, credit terms and stock availability.

The salesperson also *gets feedback* from the customer and passes it on to the company. The company can then react to this information and frame policies, amend products, improve distribution, modify advertising and change pricing.

The salesperson *solves minor problems* on the spot and prevents small sparks from becoming major fires. Most conflagrations have small beginnings. The marketplace is no different. The salesperson uses his limited authority but immediate and intimate knowledge to snuff out any problems. The country ambassador does the same.

The salesperson *creates a favourable environment* in his territory for his company and its products. This is public relations in a real sense. He is active in social circles and in community work though not at the cost of his own job. And then he finds it easier to convert people into customers in this warm and favourable environment. The ambassador does the same for his country.

The salesperson *is knowledgeable* so that he can answer questions and bridge the gaps in understanding between the corporation and the customer. He looks for areas of commonality rather than those of discord. The country ambassador tries to do this all the time.

Yes, the salesperson is an ambassador of his company, though often, salesperson do not perceive themselves in this light.

A little knowledge that acts
is worth infinitely more than
much knowledge that is idle.

—Khalil Gibran

FULCRUM OF THE ORGANISATION

The salesperson of today is the fulcrum of the company. It is he who has to sell, generate income and sustain the company.

If there are no sales, all other activities of purchase, production, administration, finance, research and development are not worth pursuing. They become useful only as a secondary activity to sales.

It is the salesperson who provides credence to Peter Drucker's accepted principle that 'the purpose of the company is to create and keep a customer'. Many salesperson do not realise this. Unfortunately, many companies do not realise this either. Some perhaps do realise, but are in no mood to accept this, especially when they are in a sellers' market and have their order books full for a year in advance.

Many salesperson, not appreciating their own significant role, want to escape from the label of 'salesperson' by trying to cloak themselves under the garb of a sales engineer, medical representative, professional sales representative, sales executive or sales officer. But they are all really doing the basic function of selling, which is a necessary and critical function. They are all salesperson.

On a Lighter Note

Raj, an ineffective salesperson, was talking about how he got started in sales.

'I started out with the theory that the selling world had an opening for me and it certainly did. I am in that hole now.'

QUESTIONS TO REFLECT ON

1. Are there any other trends that affect personal selling?
2. Would the rule of percentage be true for all products sold? Where will it not be held true?
3. What are the factors that erode a salesperson's morale?
4. Would you add any other criteria for a professional?

5. Are there any other correlations between the ambassador's job and that of a salesperson?

ACTION POINTS

1. Make a list of five customers who have changed in the last two years. Describe how they have changed.
2. What other factors (besides those noted) help to change customers?
3. Identify three salesperson you have known, where success has been the cause of failure.
4. Make a comparison between selling styles of 20 years ago and now.
5. List out the strengths in a salesperson's profile that are weaknesses in a sales manager's profile.
6. How will you prioritise the abilities of salesperson to achieve success in selling? Can you add any abilities to those already listed?
7. Can you identify salesperson you have met in the field, who have inner strength? What are the situations where they have displayed this 'tenacity'?
8. Do you have an example of a salesperson who had/implemented long-term vision?
9. Can you give an example of mentoring by a senior salesperson (like Joe in my case) from your own experience?
10. In which other professions do the practitioners need to make the last as good as the first? Why?
11. Can you list the 'demands' on the selling profession based on the brief story of Billy Lohman?
12. What do you think will be the stage after the 'stage of marketing'?
13. According to you, what can be done for salesperson to improve their level of professionalism?

CHAPTER 3

A Theory and Structure in Selling

The possession of knowledge
does not kill the sense of wonder
and mystery. There is always more mystery.

—Anais Nin

When you talk about 'selling theory' most salesperson will pooh-pooh the idea. salesperson, who have been selling for many years, are generally more resistant to the concept of selling theory. Because they belong to a generation that has been brought up to believe that selling is 'practical'. It is what happens in the field. It is very individual and cannot be generalised. And any talk of selling theory is like old wine in a new bottle.

Before we develop a negative attitude, we need to understand that theory is never sterile and never developed in isolation. All theories are derived from observations of practice. Practical incidents that can be replicated such as the falling of an apple and the displacement of water from a bathtub have given rise to the evolution of theories of gravity and of relative density.

The same principle applies to selling. From the experiences of thousands of salesperson throughout the world, some common denominators have been found and a theory has evolved. One selling process formula is AIDA (Attention, Interest, Desire, Action) —a sequence to be followed in all selling. There are other variations of this formula. There are also identified lists of common objections and standard answers to counter these objections. This book follows the AIDA formula, the objections handling system and the standard 'theory of communications'.

These theories give guidelines to new and even experienced salesperson on how to go through the selling process successfully. They need not repeat the same mistakes made by others, and can rely on and benefit from the cumulative experience of fellow professionals.

Of course, we all realise that exceptions prove the rule. Sometimes the theory may not apply. Sometimes it could be a totally new situation. The salesperson's innovative and creative abilities will be tested in these rare situations, when he will have to find new solutions to new problems.

THE AIDA FORMULA IN ACTION

Good practice always has a sound theoretical base. —Anonymous

He sits there on the pavement with his box and a transistor radio by his side. He is outside Churchgate station, Mumbai, from 8.30 in the morning, all ready to take on the avalanche of human beings who will be disgorged from the suburban trains right through the morning.

He doesn't look up at faces. He looks at the shoes. As you come by, he 'click-clacks' his box top to draw your attention, and looks you straight in the eye with the non-verbal question—'What is a man like you, doing in unpolished shoes like these?' I look at them myself, now that my attention has been drawn. I look at the time. Perhaps I have 15 minutes to spare so I can get my shoes polished. I put my foot on the shoebox. He looks up and asks, 'Cream polish?' with the same deftness as the petrol pump attendant's 'Shall I fill her up?' I nod. He has made a good sale.

He proceeds briskly, keeping up with the beat of the music. Then, a final tap. He looks at the polished shoes with satisfaction, and then looks up at me for a nod of approval. I pay and move on. As I walk away, I hear the 'click-clack' in the distance. The master craftsman is at work. In his own way he is getting attention.

Treat people if they were
what they ought to be and
you help them to become
what they are capable of being.

—Goethe

TRUST AND FAITH

The salesperson of any company, selling any product or service, must have *trust* in the company and *faith* in his product. This is the first requirement for any salesperson, irrespective of what he sells. Without this faith and trust, everything he does is doomed to failure. Why? The answer is obvious.

The salesperson begins 'selling' even before he utters the first word. His appearance, composure, expression, clothes, shoes and hair grooming will all be indicators of his confidence level. The confidence level will be high if the salesperson is proud of his company and is confident about his products. He will literally hold his head high. But with a low degree of confidence, he will virtually slink in and, having delivered his presentation, will as hastily try to slink out. The customer will not be unobservant of this. The 'fear' will be transferred from the seller to the buyer. This 'lack of confidence' is contagious.

That is why many companies spend a lot of time in classroom training—explaining the history and philosophy of the company, its policies, the way products are made, stored and distributed, shelf life, claim procedures, quality control systems, random checks in the market, and so on. Most companies reserve this input for new salesperson joining the company, as it helps to build their confidence levels. However, this should be done on an ongoing basis.

In India, quite often we have a problem. Young people join a company without finding out very much about it. They sell products about which they are told little. They are thrown into the market with little preparation. They hear criticisms of their products, their company and company policy from customers, and they cannot answer. Ultimately they lose faith in the company. They continue to sell (or try to sell) just because they have to, not because they want to, at the same time looking for another job opportunity. They are being unfair to themselves, their products, their customers and company.

That is why faith and trust are so important. To sell well and steadily you need to have firm beliefs. If you don't believe in your company and your product, it is best to quit and do something else. Because continuing to do what you do not want to do will not bring any success. However good your selling techniques may be, you just won't be able to close sales.

And if you can't close sales, you will just be making calls, not selling!

ESP FOR SUCCESSFUL SELLING

Enthusiasm, *Sincerity* and *Perseverance* (ESP) are the three pins of the socket that electrifies selling. These three qualities convert a traveller into a salesperson, a person who makes calls into a person who generates sales.

Enthusiasm

The professional salesperson believes in his product. He lives his product 24 hours of the day. It is not a chore. And when he lives his product, he feels and acts enthusiastic and consequently transmits enthusiasm. Smile, conviction and consistency are the signs of enthusiasm in a professional salesperson.

1. *Smile*: An enthusiastic salesperson is a smiling salesperson, and he spreads warmth and cheer all round. Conversely, a long-faced, grumpy salesperson is unable to sell himself and is, therefore, unlikely to sell his product and promote his company.

   The power of a smile—it can make up for other failings.

   It may seem superfluous to write about the power of a smile, yet it is such an important subject for a salesperson. After all, a smile is a non-verbal beginning of an interview. With the smile, you have already begun. Without a smile, you may not get very far.

   There are three things you should remember about smiling, if the smile is to be really effective.

   - Your teeth should be brushed and clean. Paan-stained teeth or yellowing teeth is a very unattractive sight. You may feel it does not matter but it does. The customer may not tell you, but undoubtedly, it will affect the interview.
   - Your breath should not be foul. Bad breath or the smell of tobacco or alcohol puts off customers. And yet, customers will seldom tell the salesperson about it, keeping their opinion to themselves.
   - The smile should emanate from the eyes. A smile reflected only on the lips is an insincere smile. A real smile comes

through the eyes and spreads to the mouth. Customers are adept at distinguishing a superficial smile from a genuine smile.

A company in New York runs a six-day workshop on 'smiling'. Many people attend. The fees are high. Participants are 'trained' to smile. It just shows how important smiling has become!

It is said that it takes only 18 muscles of the face to smile, and many more muscles to frown. Frowning takes up much more energy than smiling. Yet most people choose to frown. So take care when you smile and make it a clean and genuine smile.

2. *Conviction*: The professional salesperson displays conviction in his product and his product story, and makes the whole proposition credible to his customer.
3. *Consistency*: The last call of the day is as effective as the professional salesperson's first call. He does not make the last call as a bored and routine call just because 'he is here anyway'.

Sincerity

The professional salesperson is sincere. He is honest to himself and to his customer. If he finds that the product will not meet the customer's requirement as specified, he does not advise him to buy it. He does not make false claims about the product. If he is asked a question to which he has no answer, he will honestly admit this and perhaps say that he will check up with the office and revert with the answer.

The professional salesperson is looking for a continuing relationship with the customer. He is not a fly-by-night operator who wants to sell the London Bridge to an unsuspecting customer and never be seen again. Sincerity of purpose is the key to a continuing salesperson–customer relationship.

Perseverance

The professional salesperson has perseverance. He seldom gives up. When he knows that the customer has a need, or could have a need for his product, then however difficult the customer may be, he does not give up. He continues to call on him, perhaps without success.

He looks for other approaches to the customer, so that the possibility of success can increase. He displays the tenacity of Thomas Edison, who conducted 50,000 experiments before he was successful in developing the electric bulb.

> ***On a Lighter Note***
>
> A shoe salesperson who had gone on trying dozens of pairs of shoes on a fussy lady, finally asked her: 'May I pause for a few minutes please? Your feet are breaking my back.'

One's first step in wisdom is
to question everything
and one's last is to come to
terms with everything.

—Georg C. Lichtenberg

ATTENDING SELLING AND CREATIVE SELLING

There are two kinds of salesperson—attending and creative. The attending salesperson has the advantage, in that the customer comes to the shop with the intention to buy and the salesperson then satisfies his need by offering a product. This also happens in a hotel or a restaurant. The creative salesperson, on the other hand, has to go out and create a need, or unravel an existing need, and then satisfy this need with his product or service.

This does not mean that the attending salesperson does not do any creative selling at all. He does, though perhaps in a more limited way. When a customer enters a shop, and asks for a medium-size toothpaste tube, the salesperson can get him to opt for a larger economy pack of toothpaste and perhaps also sell him a toothbrush, hair cream and talcum powder. Thus he has created a need or identified a hidden need and, therefore, done the job of a creative salesperson, although he is an attending salesperson.

On a Lighter Note

Creative Selling or Buying?
The salesperson insisted on buying the worst heap from the second-hand car dealer. Car dealer: 'Why do you prefer such an old car?' Salesperson: 'When this car breaks down, a crowd will gather around me, and this will give me a chance to sell them my merchandise!'

******

Attending Selling
A man went up to the cigarette counter and asked for a brand. The clerk asked whether he wanted, 'Soft pack or crush proof box?'
'King size or regular?'
'Filter tip or plain?'
'Mentholated or minted?'
'Green pack or blue?'
Finally he asked, 'Is this charge or will you pay cash?'
The customer exclaimed: 'Forget it, I just gave up smoking!'

SELLING CONSUMER USABLES

The consumer-products salesperson may be selling matchboxes, soaps, shampoos, detergents, cooking oils or any similar product. In selling consumer usables, the creative salesperson ensures proper distribution of the product, so that when the customer is convinced of its benefits through advertising and goes to a retail outlet, the product is available and he can buy it.

The salesperson makes 30–40 visits to retailers and some to wholesalers every day. He checks the shelf stock, replenishes the stock sold and tries to get the retailer to interest himself in 'pushing' the product—because of either an additional discount or the backup of a high level of advertising and promotion, and the anticipated high turnover leading to higher profits. He also provides a service to the retailer by helping in merchandising activities. Customers will then be persuaded to buy on an impulse, having been influenced by the 'point of sale' material.

The salesperson may get into a routine where he might find his job mundane and lacking in variety. But it is really up to him to bring creativity and novelty into his seemingly 'boring' assignment.

SELLING CONSUMER DURABLES

Here again the salesperson has to ensure that the product is available at every appropriate outlet, to meet the consumer demand arising out of advertising.

However, the number of calls per day here are lower than in consumer usables because there are fewer number of outlets, which are spread further apart, and each call takes a longer time. The salesperson here needs to have more technical knowledge about the product, and should involve himself more in demonstration and merchandising.

Some salesperson of consumer durables may go door to door to meet potential customers. All their selling skills will then be required to get an entry, to draw attention, to be able to demonstrate, to create a desire to purchase and, finally, to get the customer to place an order.

Selling of consumer durables is becoming more and more competitive. It is no longer what it was 10 years ago, when there was one brand of a mixer-grinder; two of pressure cookers and refrigerators, three of electric irons, two brands of electric bulbs and ceiling fans, and another two of pedestal fans or moulded luggage. But those days are long over and companies and their field force have to face up to the grim reality that times have changed.

Therefore, now the salesperson has to be mentally more agile to know about the competition in the marketplace, and to feed this information quickly and accurately back to the company. Only then, the company can respond quickly and appropriately.

The newly introduced kitchen mixer may be priced lower, or have a bigger dealer discount, or have wider distribution, or come with some additional features for heavy duty grinding, or have a more efficient motor which does not heat up as much, or be extensively promoted, or offer longer guarantee or have a refund on old models turned in when buying a new one. The salesperson must be observant about all this and be prompt in his communication, indicating both what he has done to deal with the situation and what the company should do to deal with it.

This salesperson must be alert to find new opportunities in this highly competitive market. He must look for new territories, new outlets in existing territories and new uses if possible. This is how light bulbs are now available at bidi kiosks, moulded luggage in textile shops, and toys in general merchant outlets, cycle shops and circulating libraries. This is how plastic buckets and polyurethane shoes are sold at weekly village bazaars.

Some salesperson have been trying to push through into uncharted territories or into unconventional outlets to expand the market in order to reduce the pressure from the competition.

The consumer durables salesperson must be adept at building up strong, long-term relationships with his direct customers—stockists and retailers. Such a relationship will help considerably in keeping his market share intact and resisting encroachment by competitors into his territory or market segments.

The consumer durables salesperson must work closely with the service division of his organisation, to be able to use better service for better sales. Service must become the 'intangible plus', which adds value to the product. Alas, too often it is found that the sales and service departments work in conflict rather than in cooperation, thus destroying a significant possible advantage over the competition.

The consumer durable salesperson today must be action oriented, agile, thinking and innovative. The 'laid-back' attitude of the monopoly or oligopoly era will no longer do. It is a question of survival—succeed or perish!

SELLING SEMI-CONSUMER PRODUCTS

Pharmaceutical companies need salesperson who can promote the product personally to one group of customers (doctors) and ensure distribution by visits to another group of customers (chemists), so that finally the product is bought by the ultimate customer (patients).

The salesperson here makes fewer calls (perhaps 10 on doctors and four on chemists) and spends more time on each call with a technical discussion of his product. He will have had some technical training, so that he can meaningfully communicate with doctors, convince them and get them to prescribe. He should ensure adequate stocks at chemist outlets, so that when the prescriptions come in, they can be met.

This kind of selling—whether pharmaceuticals or pesticides—requires a greater degree of sophistication than the selling of consumer usables or consumer durables. This is because the customer is more sophisticated and knowledgeable, and the sale has to be pitched accordingly.

SELLING INDUSTRIAL CONSUMABLES

Nuts, bolts, screws, lubricating oil and similar products fall into this category. The salesperson follows the same general pattern as for consumer usables, except that in this area he will perhaps devote a large percentage of time to institutional selling, that is, getting bulk business from large users.

SELLING OF INDUSTRIAL PRODUCTS

This is a wide variety of goods from chemicals, to large-sized and expensive machinery. salesperson in this field have to be technically trained personnel with sophistication in selling. They have to be problem solvers, not just distributors and merchandisers. They have to get to know all about the customer's business, and see how their product can fulfil a need. Having thus planned in detail, they have to work out an approach and fix a meeting to show the customer how he will benefit from purchasing the product.

Selling industrial products is a long process. It can take a few months to a few years for the selling efforts to be translated into orders. In consumer products the gestation period is shorter. Again, in selling of industrial products or consumer durables, selling does not end when a sale is made. After-sales service plays a very important role in the selling process and the salesperson has to ensure that this is provided either by himself or through the company's service organisation.

Only a few years ago, all marketing activities were thought to be relevant to consumer products only. That was where the competition was, where the mass markets with millions of potential customers were, and where you needed extensive and intensive distribution, with the use of mass media like television, radio and newspapers to get your message across.

But industrial products were different. To begin with, there was hardly any competition. There were perhaps four manufacturers of paint, three of switchgear equipment; four large producers of iron ore and a few of steel. The prospective customers were few and distribution simple. The promotion was restricted to brochures and a few insertions in the trade press.

All this has changed in the new, highly competitive environment in India. The old monopolies have crumbled. India is now the

10th largest producer of industrial goods in the world. Demand has increased as has the production. Entrepreneurs are constantly looking at new opportunities. For instance, Modi diversified into tyres and ate into the market of Ceat, Dunlop, MRF and Firestone. Asian Paints came into a market dominated by Jenson and Nicholson and Goodlass, and became the largest in the field. And so it goes for spark plugs and car batteries, printing machines, textile machinery and circuit boards.

Today, the industrial product salesperson can ill afford to be 'laid-back' like in the old days—someone who is just a contact man, a public relations man for his company, a good friend who is helpful in getting priority in allocation of goods or in obtaining discounts from the company, someone who entertains all his large customers once a year and adopts a 'hail fellow, well met' attitude. Instead he has to be very knowledgeable about his product and about the competition. The industrial customer today is well educated, travels and reads a lot, and is kept well informed by the competitor's salesperson. There is greater danger that the industrial product salesperson of today, if he slackens his pace, will be overtaken not just by his competitor, but by his customer. Therefore, he must be a good observer and a good communicator to see what is going on in the marketplace and to provide feedback to the company, and communicate with the customers.

If he is selling products like cement, fertilisers and steel, he must understand logistics, distribution systems and costs. There can be large savings or losses, based on what he advises, and any error can be very costly. He must understand promotion and advertising methodology, and be innovative in using them. He must be willing to leave the beaten track and perhaps arrange farmer meetings and film shows on *haat* days to sell fertilisers, or organise group/dinner meetings for architects to sell cement.

The industrial product salesperson of today, and of the future, will really be more than a salesperson. He will need to be a marketing man, someone who studies and understands the customer and is, therefore, able to help provide a more appropriate product to the customer. It is with doing a good job in this pivotal role that his company will succeed and win over all others. All salesperson today need to convert themselves into marketing men, more so in the case of the industrial product salesperson.

SELLING SERVICES

In the marketing of services, whether hotels, transport, beauty parlours, hair saloons or any other, the salesperson plays a more critical role than in any product selling.

In services, there is nothing to show. There is something to offer—something that satisfies. If the salesperson does not have empathy, cannot tailor his offering to each customer separately and differently, and does not have the ability to follow up and check whether he has left behind a satisfied customer, then he cannot succeed in selling services.

The image of a service revolves round the salesperson, much more than in the case of a product. This is because, unlike a service, the product is something concrete and can be seen and touched.

'Selling services is different' you will be told. It is not like selling products. Services cannot really be seen or touched or heard or smelled. It does not involve the senses. So can you treat products on par with services? There are differences, yet there are many similarities. You cannot show the product, but you can show what the service can do and the satisfaction it can provide.

The medical practitioner sells a service. He cannot show it, but it can be felt over time. Unsatisfied patients cannot be provided with a replacement, as can be done with a product. The practitioner may not always be able to mend defective service although he does try. Service is based on a promise of something that will be done. A demonstration can be provided but not a sample.

Service selling, therefore, rests firmly on a skill, a promise, an experience and the evidence provided by satisfied customers. So it depends much more on people than on product selling. It depends on people who can provide the service, and those who can sell the service.

The service salesperson has to have the ability to create images, to paint pictures with words, to identify prospects and then really understand them—their hopes, their aspirations, dreams and ambitions. This is a great challenge. And those who take up this challenge are the great salesperson of this world. They are the ones who do not carry a bag of samples but have a sharp eye. They are the salespeople who sell insurance, valuation services, recruitment services, executive training programmes, taxation consultancy and management consultancy.

At a very different level, there are the shoeshine boys at railway stations; the barbers or 'tonsorial artists' at hair saloons; and the laundry services and the beauty saloon personnel. They all sell 'intangibles'. They are able to get the customer to use only a few of his senses and are, therefore, at a distinct disadvantage as compared to product salesperson. But they manage to get the customer's attention, create a desire and get him to act. In this process, they enjoy the wonderful world of selling.

MISSIONARY SALESPERSON

Some years ago, I was told about a chairman of a very large company in India, who spent all his time with a group of three well-informed advisers on planning the future of the corporation. His office was in a different city from the head office of the company. He and his group always looked 10 years ahead. They did not concern themselves with today, or this month, or even this year. The immediate future was looked after by the CEO and all the other managers and staff who managed the day-to-day affairs of the company. And the chairman always said that he would know his own effectiveness and contribution only 10 years later, and that no one would be able to judge in the present whether or not he was wasting his time.

When I think of missionary salesperson, I think about people like this chairman. Missionary salesperson are an advance force. They reconnoitre the area, look for opportunities, try and change attitudes, create a favourable environment and provide feedback. They do everything except, at times, the actual act of selling.

Missionary selling is not easy because missionary salesperson have to be pioneers. They have to overcome preconceived ideas, some prejudices and sometimes wrong notions. And this is not easy. It is the missionary salesperson who takes the message of the use of fertilisers and pesticides to areas where these have not been used in the past. It is he who takes the message of electric showers, pressure cookers, *gobar* gas systems, windmill energy generators or *sulabh shauchalaya* toilets. He has to be a master of the subject and the master of customer psychology. He has to bridge the gap between the past and the present, virtually re-enacting the initial introduction of the concept of a motor car as the 'horseless carriage' or the refrigerator as the 'electrical icebox'.

Missionary selling is not easy because missionary salesperson cannot exactly measure their contribution in terms of the day's sale. What they contribute today may bear fruit next month or next year. Sometimes they are not around to see it happen. They plant the seeds, do it as well as they can and move on. That is why they may sometimes be perceived by their colleagues as 'non-paying passengers' who are parasites on the organisation. Thus they have to contend with mental barriers not only externally in the marketplace but also among their own peers and co-workers.

Missionary salesperson need to be respected and valued. For most of us, whether we sell a product or service, the selling process has been made easier, the path cleared and the transaction facilitated by that important group whose contribution cannot be really quantified every month—the group of missionary salesperson!

QUESTIONS TO REFLECT ON

1. Would you like to convert the three-pin socket into a five-pin one?What else will you add? Why?
2. Is the salesperson's lack of confidence generally his fault, or the fault of the company? Why?
3. When is it inappropriate to smile?
4. When should a salesperson consider it prudent to 'give up'?
5. Can you develop a profile of a consumer salesperson as against that of an industrial product salesperson?
6. What are the respective criteria for labelling salesperson of consumer usables, consumer durables and industrial products?
7. Can you list any other areas of difference between product salesperson and services salesperson?

ACTION POINTS

1. Make a list of five aspects of the theory of selling with the appropriate practical applications.
2. List five salesperson you have come across who have been given good training by their companies and five others who have been let loose without any training.
3. List 10 attending salesperson and 10 creative salesperson.

4. S tudy three creative salesperson who sell different kinds of products. Write down five distinguishing characteristics for each type ofselling.
5. Describe three products that have been very successful because they have focussed on providing excellent after-sales service.
6. Describe the contributions made by missionary salesperson in at least three industries.

CHAPTER 4

Planning for the Sale

Lot of folks confuse bad management with destiny.

—Kim Hubbard

The professional salesperson today is a 'thinker' in addition to being a 'doer'. He does not rush out like a bull in a china shop. He begins with a plan. He finds out whom he has to see, where and when, and estimates what he hopes to achieve. This kind of planning makes him a professional—a real salesperson who sells.

It is said that in a highly competitive environment, the salesperson, especially in industrial products, may spend 30 per cent of his time in planning and 70 per cent in implementing. If he does not do this, there is a danger that 100 per cent of field work will yield only 30 per cent productivity.

The thinking and planning salesperson should then be distinguished from a traveller, who only makes calls. The traveller is not concerned whether these calls result in sales or not. If the sales are not commensurate with the expenses, then the traveller blames the advertising, the after-sales service, the quality of the product, the pricing and distribution, but he does not re-examine the quality of his selling. Thus the wide 'attitude divide' between salesperson and travellers.

On a Lighter Note

There is the story about a man who was told if he worked very hard he would become very rich. The hardest work he knew was

(Continued)

(Continued)

> digging holes, so he set about digging holes in his backyard. He didn't get rich, he only got a backache. He worked hard, but he worked without a purpose.

OFFER SOMETHING NEW

How often have we heard customers ask the salesperson as soon as the greetings are over: 'So what's new?' or 'Anything new?' or words to that effect. And all of us know that we can never have something new on every visit. Most times, it is the same old products with the same old features and advantages. If there is nothing new for the customer and, also for the salesperson, then the 'spark' of enthusiasm will be missing in the interview. The salesperson will actually be bored with his job and, therefore, look and act bored.

There is an old saying that 'beauty lies in the eyes of the beholder'. The newness in the selling situation lies in the eyes of the salesperson. Only he can bring freshness to the selling situation. But he can only do it if he really wants to.

In this context it is worth looking at the story of Joe who sold cars for more years than he could remember. 'Didn't you ever get bored selling only cars for so many years Joe?' people asked.

'Never,' he said, 'because no two presentations are ever the same. There is always a variety of automobiles to sell. There are numerous new models every year. But more than that, no two prospects are ever the same.'

A salesperson today cannot do a decent job without being armed with an arsenal of different 'closes', which he uses according to what develops during a sales presentation.

The days are gone when you could use one standard 'close' on everybody. While one 'close' may work perfectly for the prospect who complains that he can't afford to buy, another may work for the procrastinator who wants to talk it over with his wife. Yet another is perfect for the person who is a compulsive shopper.

Joe also said that he dreaded to think how poor his sales career would have been if he had sold cars with only one type of 'close'. He added, for the record, that the majority of his sales were made after the first closing attempt had failed. There is a lesson in Joe's story for all of us. There is always something new, provided we take the trouble to find it.

STRIKE EMPATHY

In today's complex marketplace, the professional salesperson does more homework than he did in the past to clearly define the customer profile: What kind of a person is he? What is his background, level of education, career path and temperament? What are his interests, hobbies, strong points and weaknesses, needs and wants?

All this knowledge helps him to strike empathy with the customer, to put himself in the customer's shoes and look at a problem from the customer's point of view. Then he can tailor his message in such a way that the customers see the problem from his point of view.

Striking empathy helps the salesperson to gain trust. Without trust there can be no continuity in sales. The customer must trust the salesperson and, consequently, the product and the company. The salesperson can do this successfully only if he develops an open mind, where he genuinely likes his customers and is sincere about their welfare. Liking begets liking. It is difficult to dislike someone who likes you. And this makes a successful salesperson, one who does not sell but makes the customer want to buy his product.

TARGET FOR THE HEART

Prof. Philip Kotler, one of the world's best marketing gurus, while on a short visit to India some time ago, was asked at a seminar, 'How can you get a customer to choose one computer from all the other competing brands, when all these brands are virtually identical?' Kotler explained that in many product categories we might have come to a stage where product differentiation is virtually impossible, where there is a large number of similar products—identical in design, colour, performance and price. An innovator is quickly followed by a large number of imitators. What can one then do?

There is something that the company can do. It can differentiate its product from those of its competitors, in ways external to the product itself—perhaps in distribution, or in advertising and promotion, or for many products, like computers, in the kind of salespersons they employ, train and motivate to sell the product.

The customer will buy from that salesperson who is knowledgeable, who gives him service, is pleasant and, above all, has taken the time and trouble to understand his needs and wants, and then tried to fit the product into that need. All other things being equal, the customer will buy from such a salesperson. This is what will distinguish the successful product from its less successful competitors.

Most salesperson know this theory. It is a pity that they forget to put this theory into practice. Because to put it into practice requires a lot of self-discipline and genuine 'love' for the customer. A computer salesperson needs to spend time with the junior staff at the prospects' offices to find out their problems and needs. An equipment salesperson needs to spend time with the blue-collar workers on the factory floor to find out their problems and their opinions. A medical representa- tive needs to visit chemist shops to find out the prescribing habits of doctors in the neighbourhood. A consumer product salesperson needs to spend time unobtrusively at the shop counter to observe what customers are asking for, and perhaps to find out why.

But all this has to come out of the salesperson's own time. He does not get 'credit' for it. He cannot show this extra work as extra calls. If he genuinely loves his work and loves his customers, and wants to serve rather than just sell, he will go through all this extra labour. In the long run, the results will reflect this extra input, and customers will prefer his product, even though there are others which are identical ones. These are salesperson who are professional, and who *target for the heart of the customer*.

> *To be conscious that you are ignorant,*
> *is a great step to knowledge.*
>
> —Disraeli

SELECT TERRITORIES AND CUSTOMERS

This is a critical decision area for the modern salesperson. Which areas should he cover? And within an area, which potential customers should he contact? How often? In what manner and for how long?

There may be territories which are not worth covering because they will not give reasonable returns for the salesperson's time, effort and money. The salesperson may decide to visit a territory every week or every fortnight, every month or two months or once in six months or a year. Within the area, the salesperson will decide about potential buyers in the same way, whether they are to be contacted every week, once a year or at any frequency in between. Customers in some low potential territories may be covered only by mailings or by telephone—the frequency of contact based on the potential.

Planning Work—Working the Plan

Yogesh was a smart, presentable and poor 14-year-old who had come to the big city of Mumbai from a small village 200 miles away. Like many others, he found that the streets were not paved with gold. It was a hard task, just to keep alive in Mumbai.

I got acquainted with him when I drew my car to the kerb on Peddar Road, with a flat tyre. He came up to sell me a book with race tips. It was then that I enquired about his modus operandi. He sold the book from Wednesday to Saturday. He operated only between Marine Drive and the Turf Club, a distance of 3 miles. He contacted only private car drivers who were driving in the direction towards the Turf Club. He ensured that other booksellers were not too close by.

His market segmentation was as best as it could be. He had given the matter considerable thought. Since his planning and execution were both good, he sold at least 40 books a day. 'The more calls I make, the better results I get,' he said, and it certainly made sense.

> ***On a Lighter Note***
>
> At the conclusion of an inspirational sales meeting, the salesperson rushed out and hailed a taxi. 'Where to?' the cab driver asked him. 'Take me anywhere, I have prospects everywhere!' he replied.

CLASSIFY CUSTOMERS

The professional salesperson knows how to place his customers in categories, in the same way as purchase and production managers classify stores into A, B and C categories. Customers with the most potential belong to category A, while those with the least belong to C. This categorisation is not a reflection on the customer as a person, but of the volume and frequency at which they will buy. The A-customers will perhaps be the busiest and the most difficult to meet. And yet they are the ones who need to be met most often, and the meeting period in their case should be the longest.

Even a few A-customers in a remote town may make the town an A-town. After all, the potential of the town is dependent on the potential of the prospective customers who live there. Towns are then classified like customers, based on customers in those towns. The salesperson then decides how often to visit each town and meet each customer. In doing this, he follows the basic principles of time management. The C-customer who is expanding rapidly and has the potential to become an A-customer must also be visited frequently, as often as an A-customer.

Customer classification is always based on today's needs as well as long-term possibilities. In all this, the salesperson needs to use judgement and understanding. He needs to be a territory manager.

Taking the product to the Customer

Bombay Hospital at New Marine Lines in Mumbai has excellent facilities for the treatment of cardiac patients. Many of them are recommended coconut water so as to give them an intake of potassium, in palatable form.

Ramesh sits on the pavement outside the hospital, doing brisk business every morning, selling coconuts for the many takers there. He has been there for 12 years now, with a steady and growing business, at a location which he had selected after 'identifying his target buyers' using his own 'common sense'.

On a Lighter Note

Confucius say: 'The salesperson who covers chair instead of territory, always remains at the bottom.'

IDENTIFY INFLUENCERS, DECIDERS, PURCHASERS AND USERS

The biggest stumbling block to good selling is that salesperson do not identify the right person to meet.

Every salesperson on every sales call must be able to identify the MAN—the person who has the Money, the Authority and the Need. He must be able to research and to find out

- who can *initiate* the decision;
- who can *influence* it;
- who can *decide*;
- who will be the formal *purchaser*; and
- who will be the *user*.

It is easy when all these roles are performed by one person. But most times, especially in industrial selling and in large corporations, these roles are performed by different persons, or even groups of persons. Research is necessary to find out who the gatekeepers are (the secretary or the receptionist), who influences a decision, who decides, who actually purchases and who uses.

Millions of rupees are wasted every month through salesperson making calls on people who do not have a need, will not have a need, do not have the money or do not have the authority to buy.

The Elusive MAN in Selling

The telex dictionary (TD) published in 1980 was the first of its kind in the world. Its use could save a company at least 20 per cent on telex bills every month, with shorter words, phrases and internationally accepted abbreviations. The price was small, as compared to the savings which would accrue to a company. There was no need for re-learning or retraining the telex operators. And yet the telex dictionary did not sell, or did not sell as much as was expected.

The salesperson Sheila met the telex operators and explained the product benefits. They were not interested in saving money for the corporation. And there was the natural resistance to anything new. 'We have managed quite well without the TD, all these years,' they said.

Sheila tried meeting the managing directors and finance directors. They would not meet because granting an interview to someone who has come to sell a TD was a criminal waste of executive time.

The critical combination of factors—MAN (Money, Authority and Need)—was missing. The operators neither felt the need nor had the authority. The directors had the authority, but did not make the time to see the need. And the marketing of the TD was a big failure.

> *On a Lighter Note*
>
> A salesperson said to his wife one evening: 'I'm glad I'm not in business for myself. I wasted the whole day.'

DERIVE A CALL LIST AND A JOURNEY PLAN

The salesperson can now work out his call list. This lists the potential customers and identifies where they are located, how often they should be met and what will be achieved at each meeting. Based on this knowledge, he estimates his sales achievement in each area and works out his journey plan, marking towns or areas against each date of the month.

Work out the Daily Plan

The daily plan of work lists the customers to be met on each day, the topics to be discussed and the products to be sampled or demonstrated. The salesperson's bag contains all available materials—price list, order book, product literature, demonstration kit and reference material—arranged in such a way that he can pick out what he wants, without looking in and groping in the middle of the sales conversation.

The salesperson should be well groomed—hair in place, neatly shaved, clean clothes and polished shoes. Nothing loud and nothing to detract the customer's primary focus from the product to the salesperson! He should also decide on the manner in which the contact will be made. Sometimes a telephone call may be sufficient, either as an introductory call or as a reminder call. Sometimes a letter through the mail may serve the purpose, at other times, a brief personal visit or a long, protracted discussion may be required. This decision depends on both the product being sold and the customer profile.

> *On a Lighter Note*
>
> The salesperson asked the receptionist, 'When is the best time to see the purchase manager?'
>
> She replied, 'Before lunch, his mind is irritable, and after lunch, his stomach is irritable.'

How Planning Helps

A salesperson for an oil company was calling on a small plant in south India. He was a friendly sort, and his winning manner electrified the young lady who presided over the reception desk. She called the purchasing agent. Again the salesperson made good use of his friendly manner. They chatted a minute about the weather and then the salesperson showed the purchasing agent some samples of certain oils and greases, asking for a trial order.

'I appreciate your dropping in,' said the bored purchasing agent, 'but we don't need anything in your line right now. However, you might check with the superintendent if you want to go through the trouble.'

The salesperson thanked the purchasing agent and went to meet the superintendent. Again he turned on his personal charm and had a pleasant interview. The superintendent assured him that he would keep him in mind. The salesperson left, feeling pleased with himself, quite sure that some day his call might bear fruit.

Later that day, the salesperson for a competitive oil company called on the same firm. He politely asked to see the superintendent by name. It was quite evident he had something definite on his mind. When he met the superintendent, he said: 'I understand Mr Narayan that you have had two breakdowns on that main drive shaft in the past week, and I think I know the answer. May I have your permission to check the oil cups and see what kind of lubrication the bearings are getting?'

The superintendent was interested at once. He did not know how the salesperson knew about the breakdowns, but he was interested in any practical suggestion to prevent a recurrence of the trouble. They found that the oil being used was too heavy to flow freely into the bearings, with the result that the bearings ran hot. The salesperson left with an order for a drum of lubricating oil that would flow more freely and at a price considerably more than the company had been paying earlier.

QUESTIONS TO REFLECT ON

1. What do you think should be the time allocated to planning for salesperson of consumer usables, durables, industrial products and services?

2. Should all planning be done mentally or is there a need to write down the plan? Why?
3. Is it always possible to bring in something new at the sales interview? If not, then what will you do?
4. What is the difference between apathy, sympathy and empathy? Should a salesperson also use other sentiments sometimes, besides empathy? If yes, in which situations?
5. Is appealing to the heart more important than appealing to the mind? What would be the emphasis?
6. In your own work, how can you 'target for the heart' for different categories of customers?
7. Can the selection of customers and territories, customer classification, call list and journey plan make the salesperson's work too structured and thus reduce creativity?
8. Is there really a need for a daily work plan? Why? What are the advantages of unplanned flexibility?

ACTION POINTS

Analyse the territory you need to cover according to the following instructions.

1. List the total number of prospective customers (prospects). Based on the potential of each, classify into the following categories:
   A: High potential
   B: Medium potential
   C: Low potential
   Then derive a customer classification chart.
2. Decide the frequency at which you will make calls:
   A: Every 15 days
   B: Every 30 days
   C: Every 60 days
   Then derive a call frequency chart.
3. Decide whether you will follow the Pie System of travel (complete circuit before returning to the HQ), or the Petal System of travel (smaller trips and return to HQ frequently). Then derive the tour plan or journey plan, incorporating the date, town and mode of travel.

4. Prepare a daily work plan for the town:
   Whom will you see?
   What will you promote?
   What will you say?
   How will you say it?
   What do you expect to achieve, i.e., what is the objective?
   Name of Customer/Products Promoted/Literature Given/Samples Given/Follow-up Required/Remarks
5. Prepare the sales kit.
   Is the bag in good condition? Is it polished?
   Does it contain the following:
      Diary
      Tour Plan
      Customer profile card
      Relevant literature
      References
      Company brochure
      Relevant samples
      Demonstration kit
      Visiting cards
      Order Book/Pen
      Any other material useful in merchandising

   Always keep the bag on the side across from the customer (unless you are facing the customer squarely). Never keep the bag on the table or on the chair next to you.

Chapter 5

Self-Management in Selling

Try not be become a man of success
but rather try to become a man of value.

—Albert Einstein

In no other profession is self-management as necessary as in selling. It distinguishes the professional from the traveller. The salesperson is out in the field, all on his own, for most of the year. Unlike personnel in the office, there are no timings to be kept, no personal surveillance is possible. Even his sales supervisor can perhaps meet him once or twice a month, for a day or two at a time. The salesperson can decide either to be professional or be consigned to the general category of 'traveller'.

The professional salesperson does not need to be managed by a sales manager. He manages himself. He therefore gives careful thought to the territory he will cover, the category of customers he will see, who he will meet, what exactly he will discuss, what he expects to achieve and how he will close the interview. He then follows it up on his own to find out whether his call on a doctor has resulted in prescriptions at the chemist shop or if his call on the farmer has resulted in sales at the pesticide dealer. If not, he will make repeat calls and continue calling until he has achieved success.

This is the reason why the professional salesperson spends some time in writing reports. He does not find this to be a burden. He does not ask the usual traveller's question, 'Am I paid to sell, or to sit and write reports'. The salesperson realises that reports can be written during waiting periods in between calls. They can then be consolidated quickly and completely, at the end of the day. These reports reflect the salesperson's communication ability and help him to

- analyse his own work in retrospect;
- keep a record as guidelines for the future;
- convey to his office the progress he is making in his work.

This is self-management in salespersonship. Once a salesperson has mastered the art of self-management, he has arrived as a professional salesperson.

On a Lighter Note

Ineffective salesperson: 'Will I be getting a raise soon?'
Sales manager: 'Of course, you will be getting a raise, and it will be effective just as soon as you are.'

A MARKETING MAN

The salesperson of the 21st century must understand the total concept of marketing—all activities involved in providing customer satisfaction at a profit, making optimum use of available resources. In some ways, the term salesperson may be a misnomer in the present market environment. Today's salesperson is a marketing man. He is not just selling. He is, or should be, doing far more than that.

He is really the company's primary market investigator. He studies the changing market environment, the changing customer attitudes, new competition and preferences, so that he can then give this feedback to his company. This will enable the company to gear itself for introducing new products/services to meet new market needs, and to take action to fight new competition. The company can also take other actions such as modifying products or packaging, changing prices, distribution methods or promotion strategies, thereby delaying product obsolescence and, consequently, protecting or expanding its market share.

In many companies, salesperson do not play this expanded role, which would enrich their job. They do not gain a 'helicopter' vision. On the contrary, they remain order takers or hustlers and, in the process, fall into a routine, get bored and then opt out or get thrown out. All this while, the possibilities remain untapped, unfortunately for themselves and for the company.

Sometimes, companies are to be blamed for not encouraging their salesperson to expand their horizons. There is no reaction or reply to the reports and observations sent to the marketing office. Salesperson wonder if their reports are read at all. Or worse, someone higher up in the marketing office takes credit for the suggestion made by the salesperson, and walks away with recognition and the prize.

> *Knowledge is like money*
> *the more he gets, the more he craves.*
>
> —Josh Billings

ONGOING MARKET RESEARCH

The salesperson can do regular market research much better and more economically than a market research agency. He does not have to familiarise himself with the market as he already knows his product and the competition. He can see many more customers and cover a bigger geographical area and is more competent to analyse the results. On the other hand, the investigator from the research company has to start from scratch.

The only disadvantage is that the salesperson may have preconceived ideas and may not be objective. He must not allow the findings to be coloured by what he believes, but report his observations accurately. Based on these findings, he can perhaps make suggestions and recommend a course of action.

The market research agency can then be used for special projects, maybe a special survey for a proposed product, for a purchase motivation study or other such situations.

But regular ongoing market research must be the part-assignment of the marketing person who is generally known as the salesperson.

What market research entails for the salesperson

- Extra legwork and more time in the marketplace
- Meeting more customers and a greater variety of customers
- More prospecting
- Spending more time at sales counters to observe what happens at the point of sale
- Ability to ask questions and listen
- Constantly looking for leads to new ideas, new opinions and new customers
- Developing acute powers of observation

- Developing a certain objectivity so that the opinions are not coloured by having your nose too close to the ground
- Developing an analytical ability to convert information into knowledge
- Developing a quick feedback system to the office so that remedial action is taken
- Ability to be continuously on the ball because change is taking place all the time

> *On a Lighter Note*
>
> A radio rating agency phoned a thousand men to ask:
> 'Who are you listening to right now?'
> Eighty-five per cent replied: 'My wife.'

How market research helps the salesperson

- It takes the salesperson beyond the monotonous routine of making sales calls and writing orders.
- It improves his abilities from being a 'sales' man to being a 'marketing' man.
- It expands his vision and sharpens his perspective of the job.
- It increases his ability to provide feedback so he can make suggestions and recommend a course of action.
- It improves his ability to plan and thus be more productive in his job.
- It increases his ability to take independent action, to research the competition and show how his product is better and/or more economical.

All this converts the salesperson from a drone into a queen bee.

Hints for effective market research

1. *Be objective* by not allowing the findings to be coloured by what you believe.
2. *Be creative* in your analysis. Be like Sherlock Holmes.
   - For example, worn-out floor tiles in front of the hatching chick exhibit at Chicago's Museum of Science and Industry

showed the management that it was the museum's most popular exhibit.

- Think about the problem and don't just rely on databases and reports. While these are important, they should make you think further and not limit your thinking.
- Like Holmes, see and understand relationships among seemingly unrelated facts.
- Develop your own information sources—sometimes many of these are available within your own company.

The ability to be two steps ahead

It was not a very large shop at Majestic Circle, Bengaluru. But the attractive display of footwear in the show window and the large satin banner announcing a 10 per cent introductory discount on the latest sports footwear caught my attention.

We went in, to be greeted by a salesperson who, we later discovered, was the proprietor. He showed us the different designs, told us what he would recommend, tried on different pairs on me and my two sons. Finally we asked for the prices. Then we got up and said we will have to think about it. 'Why?' he asked. We told him we had seen similar shoes on the pavement on Brigade Road last night, being sold for 60 per cent of the price now being quoted. 'Yes,' he said, 'that's right.' Then very briefly he showed us the quality points of the shoes he was selling, and how these were absent in the shoes that we mentioned, but which 'seemed' to look the same. He also told us the names of the better known shops in the more sophisticated area of the city, where the same quality of shoes would be available, but at prices 20 per cent higher because of the location.

He had his data on his fingertips, knowledge of his product and of his competitors. He inspired confidence in the customer. We asked him to pack the three pairs, paid the bill and walked out.

SALES FORECASTER FOR HIS AREA

The professional salesperson is also the sales forecaster for his area. Since he knows his area best, he alone can best assess the potential and the prospects. The company's responsibility is to provide him with past sales data, general economic indicators, proposed inputs of effort, information on new products to be introduced, experiences in other similar territories and other such details. The salesperson can then work out what can be achieved with these inputs, based on his knowledge of the territory.

The sales manager compiles all this data received from the salesperson in his area and presents this to the marketing manager, who then presents it to the general manager. Thus, forecasting becomes an exercise starting from grassroots, rather than a target imposed from above, with perhaps no rational basis. It also becomes a participative exercise, an example of management by objectives. This is where each salesperson works out for himself an achievable but ambitious and rational target, and then tries to achieve it, like a high jumper setting his own bar and then trying his best to see how far he can go.

This preferred method of target setting needs two prerequisites: an objectivity on part of the salesperson, who should not be trying to set a target that is the lowest and easiest to achieve, and an open mind on part of the company, so that it spells out its plans and requirements in clear terms for the salesperson to have sufficient data to work on.

MANAGER OF HIS TIME

The professional salesperson is an excellent manager of time. Since this is a field job, he has full flexibility. He can start late and finish early. There are no fixed timings like in an office. He can therefore use his time or waste it. It is very important that the salesperson knows how to use his time to get the best results.

The professional salesperson plans so that he spends as much time as possible in meeting the customers, and as little as possible in travelling between seeing customers. He plans his journey cycle from one town to another accordingly, and within the town, from one customer to another, based on their location and the time at which they are most easily available.

He follows a basic tour programme or journey cycle, not because the company can check on him, but because the company then knows how and where to contact him if there is an emergency. It is like leaving a copy of your programme at home, when going on a trip out of town.

He generally adopts one of the two systems in his journey plan. One is called the Pie System where he moves right around the territory and then comes back to the starting point. The other is the Petal System where he keeps coming back to the base point. Either way, it is a system, one which helps to achieve the objective of maximum contact time and minimum travel time.

FINDING TIME

Many salesperson find that the biggest problem today is finding the time to do everything. There never seems to be enough time between starting out in the morning, rushing for a bus or train, standing in endless queues, being kept waiting for long periods by customers, sometimes spending hours in non-business idle chatter with customers, braving heat, cold or rain and, finally, heading home at the end of a working day, maybe at 6 in the evening or 11 at night. The same long queues again and travelling in cramped trains/ buses to return like a wet rag, too tired to do anything but retire as soon as possible, to be fit for another day, to be fit for tomorrow. And so the wheel turns.

Where is the time to do professional reading, to write daily reports, expense statements, special market reports or customer cards? There is never enough time, unless you find the time or create the time. Most people in any profession, who take their jobs seriously and try to achieve excellence, have the same problem. They are always rushed for time. Yet this is generally an excuse. If you analyse any working day, you will find that right through the day you waste a lot of time in small fragments, which when totalled work out to many hours, perhaps three or four hours in a day.

If you will only take the trouble to carry a book on selling or marketing and your blank report forms with you all the time, you can utilise the time waiting to see customers in either reading and improving your mind, or in writing up details of the earlier call and getting this chore out of the way. Instead of this, most salesperson will spend the time gazing vacantly at the passing scene, or daydreaming, or carrying out idle chatter with other salesperson also waiting or smoking. They then find out that the day is gone and similarly the week. There is a lot of accumulated report work to be then done at the weekend, which becomes cumbersome. And then again, there is no time for serious professional reading.

For a salesperson it is important to save and use the snippets of time between calls. You can get at least three hours of useful work done every day, which is 54 hours a month. A saving of two full days a month means three weeks in a year. Try this. It can be an important first step to achievement and excellence.

> *On a Lighter Note*
>
> Sales manager: 'No wonder you can't find time to eat, sleep and call on prospects. Look at all the miles you have driven according to your expense account.'

THE COST OF A SALES CALL

When someone goes to a movie or to the theatre and is disappointed, the normal reaction is to think of the waste of time and money. That is why most people take some trouble to read reviews and check with friends whether the movie is worth going to. It could be a matter of just Rs 100–200, yet people are very careful.

Each sales call can cost anything from Rs 100 to Rs 5000, depending on whether one is selling a mass distributed consumer product or a very high value heavy engineering item. Yet, one can be quite careless in the initial preparation, getting the background and tailoring the selling presentation and strategy to ensure success. A salesperson can get into a boring routine. Sometimes he makes it so obvious that he is bored with his job, his product and his company that even his customer wonders why the salesperson called in the first place. For every salesperson, a good technique to adopt is to think of the cost of every sales call before entering any customer's office. It helps him to do his best. Even if he does not get the order, it does not matter. He knows that he did his best.

Always bear in mind
that your own resolution to succeed
is more important than any other thing.

—Abraham Lincoln

WHY SALESPERSON FAIL

It is said that many salesperson throughout the world fail to become professional salesperson because of some of the following five reasons:

1. They are overconfident of their own methods and do not want to change. They feel thy alrady knw enough. The longer they have been in the field, the more complacent they tend to get and, therefore, more resistant to change.
2. They blame every lost sale on some other factors but never on their own sdling techniques. There are floods or there is a drought, the competition is great or the price is high. But their own selling techniques are never analysed and corrected.
3. When the customer says 'I'll think about it' or 'Let me see', or makes some other non-committal comment, the salesperson still feels happy that he may get the order, and goes away quite content. He has no right to be. He should only be happy if he has got the order on his pad.
4. Salesperson often take the customer for granted. They feel they have the customer 'in their pocket' and the latter will unswervingly remain loyal to the salesperson, and to his product and company. They feel they are great psychologists. In taking their customers for granted, they lose them.
5. Salesperson rely too little on planning. Generally they improvise. In this process they take longer to do a job and do it badly. Planning simplifies implmentation. But many salesperson feel that planning is something theoretical and has no place in the practical realms of sales skills.

On a Lighter Note

Inefficient salesperson: 'I'm sure that business is picking up. I'm starting to lose bigger sales.'

******

One sales manager said to a fired salesperson: 'In a way though, I'll be sorry to lose you. You've been like a son to me—insolent, surly and unappreciative.'

QUESTIONS TO REFLECT ON

1. Can a salesperson really work as a marketing man, within the limits of his authority? What areas of marketing would be beyond the scope of his influence?

2. What are the different methods of market research? Which method will you use and in which situations?
3. What are the advantages and disadvantages of each method?
4. The sales forecasting system suggested in this chapter is too time-consuming. Do you agree? Is there any way this can be done faster and as well?
5. Can you list, in order of priority, all the time-wasting activities for a salesperson?
6. Doyouknowanythingabout'assertiveness'?Inwhichsituations will you use 'assertiveness' with customers, colleagues or friends in the field?
7. I n a system where daly contact with the sales office is required, how can you reduce the time spent on travelling and in meeting/reporting?
8. What expertise should a salesperson pick up to help him save time?
9. Can you add any more reasons to those listed of why experienced salesperson sometimes fail?

ACTION POINTS

For every customer you intend to call on, you need to understand in advance the following:

1. What does he buy—your product or the competitor's?
2. Why does he buy?
   - Need
   - Keeping up with others
   - Psychological satisfaction
3. Who among the following (one or more) does the buying?
   - Gatekeeper
   - Initiator
   - Influencer
   - Decider
   - Purchaser
   - User
4. When does he buy—season and time?
5. Where does he buy—from the Internet, the retailer or a TV shopping network?
6. How much does he buy?
7. How does he pay—cash, credit or part payment?

You can find answers to these questions from a secondary or primary data collection. Secondary data is published data which is easily available, though sometimes outdated. It includes data from government statistics, yellow pages and trade directories.

Primary data can be collected through observation (just standing at shop counters, i.e., point of sale), through experiment (changing the shop displays and correlating with how this affects sales) and through surveys (through telephone, mail or personal meetings).

Based on answers to these questions and the benefits of the product which will be of interest to a particular customer, formulate a sales presentation to be made, right from the initial greeting to the close.

Make sure that you present all the material you have learnt by heart in a natural and conversational tone. That is the mark of a great salesperson. Call on the customer at a time most convenient to him, even if not necessarily convenient to you.

CHAPTER 6

Focussing on the Customer

> *To give real service you must add something which cannot be bought or measured with money, and that is sincerity and integrity.*
>
> —Douglas Adams

The salesperson will generally succeed if he makes the customer feel like a star. To do this, he has to study the customer.

1. What kind of a person is he?
2. What is his background?
3. What is his temperament?
4. What are his interests?
5. What is his business?
6. What are his plans?
7. What are his needs?
8. What could be his needs/wants?

How can you help him? If you put together the answers to all these questions, you can really strike empathy with the customer. You can sell. If you don't, then you cannot strike a chord with the customer. You make calls, but perhaps don't sell.

Empathy is the ability to see the problem from the customer's point of view. It is also the ability to get the customer to see your own point of view. Most of the time the problem is that the salesperson makes himself the star and either talks down to the customer or talks on a different wavelength. There is then no communication or empathy, and, therefore, no sale.

> *On a Lighter Note*
>
> A salesperson decided one day that he had enough of selling. He was going to switch jobs. He became a policeman.
>
> Many months later, a former colleague met him on the road and asked how he liked his new job.
>
> 'Great,' said the salesperson, 'what I like best about it is that the customer is always wrong.'

'I KNEW IT ALREADY'

'I knew it already' is the one sentence that is used often by well-informed salesperson everywhere. And yet, it is a sentence which should be used the least by salesperson who know and realise that it is their duty to make the customer a 'star'.

Sometime back I was present at an interview where a medical representative (MR) was talking to a doctor, introducing a new product of his company. Soon after he started, the doctor said that he had read about the product a few months ago in some medical journal published in the UK. So he already knew something about Benzone. The MR immediately took the bait, instead of letting it pass. 'Yes,' he said, 'to be precise, it appeared in the 5 October issue of the Lancet. =In fact, I have a reprint here in my bag. Would you like to keep a copy for your reference?'

The doctor looked so deflated. He leaned back in his chair, crossed his arms and lost interest in whatever followed. The MR lost a golden opportunity of making the customer a star. He put his own ego above the customer's. He wanted to show that he was himself well-read. Instead of making an impression, he lost a customer, not only for Benzone, but perhaps for his other products as well.

What should the MR have done? He should have looked surprised. He should have let the doctor talk. He should have said that the drug had been mentioned somewhere, but that he did not know the details. He should have subtly complimented the doctor on his up-to-date information and knowledge of everything important appearing in the medical world, and mentioned that every interview with him was an opportunity to learn something. He should have further encouraged the doctor to talk so that he would have detailed the product to himself, and the MR would not have had to do very much more.

Such an approach requires self-control. It requires self-discipline. It requires a constant reminder that the customer is the king. And that the smart salesperson's job is to make the customer a 'star'—to purposely take second place, even when he knows that he could be first. There are no exceptions to this rule.

When the general merchant tells the soap company salesperson the test cricket score, which the salesperson already knows, he has to look surprised, thank him for the information and ask for more. The general merchant then feels superior—the power derived from knowledge—and then looks at the salesperson more favourably. The sales engineer, on being told by the vice president, operations, what he heard about the proposed import duties in the new budget, should not say that he read something about it in the last issue of *Business World*. He will be wise to listen attentively and go on from there.

Whatever you sell, at whatever customer level you sell, the general rule remains the same. Make the customer a star. And you will never be able to do this if you say 'I knew it already'.

> *On a Lighter Note*
>
> A wife with an armful of clothes parcels, on returning from the shopping trip told her husband: 'A salesgirl at the shop could not understand why a glamorous woman like me was not in the films.'

NON-VERBAL COMMUNICATION

Of all the aspects of body language that we are aware of, the following aspects are those which will make other people think of us as attractive.

1. *Eye Contact*: In some countries of South East Asia and the Middle East, eye contact, especially between males and females, is not encouraged. In today's world of globalisation, it will do us well to remember that in the West, poor eye contact indicates that the person is not very open and honest. So maintain as much eye contact, as is comfortable for you. While staring is to be avoided, more eye contact is likely to lead to greater liking,

greater awareness and more accurate understanding of the other's body language. We have to remember that communication is as much a question of accurate reception of signals as it is of skilful transmission. The size of the pupil is a useful indicator of liking. Since it is beyond conscious control, it can be more revealing than many other aspects of body language.

2. *Facial expression*: This should be lively rather than too carefully controlled and restricted. Our facial expressions provide others with information about us, information that is more likely to provoke a favourable response. Even unattractive people can appear attractive if they have lively and expressive faces. Many comedians are ugly or have odd-looking faces, yet their faces are usually so expressive that their ugliness almost becomes a kind of beauty.
3. *Head movements*: Use single and double head nods to encourage others to speak and to show attention on your part. Head nods can help an encounter progress smoothly. The more you encourage other people to talk, the more they will like you. Not that you should content yourself with being a permanent listener, but you should seek to share the floor and avoid hogging it.
4. *Gestures*: As Indians, we often speak with our hands. We should be expressive but not overdo it. Perhaps the best way would be to keep hands out of our pockets, avoid arm-folding and other 'barrier' gestures. Gestures should be open and expressive, not contrived and affected. Just let them flow as a natural accompaniment both to the rest of your body language and to what you say.
5. *Posture*: When standing, be reasonably erect. Lean forward when trying to convey active interest and involvement. However, there are times when a backward leaning, asymmetrical posture will help maintain an informal atmosphere.
6. *Proximity and orientation*: Approach as closely as you can, without embarrassing others. Every person is comfortable about the space around them. If any other person 'invades' this space by coming too close, the person feels threatened. Try it for yourself, and see. Usually a space of around 1.5 feet around a person is what would be considered 'their personal territory'.

7. *Body contact*: Touch as often as you can, without being offensive. Indian males are comfortable walking down the streets hand in hand, or with an arm around each other. Westerners view this as odd. Touch is a wonderful method of non-verbal communication when used properly, e.g., when a person is going through a difficult time or has lost a loved one. Just a handshake and eye contact can be more expressive than words. Handshakes, arm pats, shoulder pats and guiding hands are contacts that may be safe to start with. But, care needs to be exercised here and progress in using body contact should be dictated by what others find appropriate. It is more a question of following others' initiatives, rather than taking too much of a lead.
8. *Appearance and physique*: Dress according to group norms, but go for colour where you can—this is more pertinent to lady salespersons, rather than men. Keep slim. In today's world a high value is placed on slimness and the overweight should seriously consider slimming down, or dressing in ways that disguise the extra flab.
9. *Non-verbal aspects of speech*: Do not talk too much or too fast but try to talk as well as listen, in roughly equal proportions. People like listeners. You will have to balance the two. Control volume, pitch and tone to suit the environment. Aim for a reasonably standard accent, and try and overcome regional extremes.

   Once you are aware of the characteristics of your own speech, perhaps by listening to a tape of yourself, you can exercise some control. Avoid speaking too loudly or with too harsh a tone. Avoid speaking too rapidly and avoid 'umms', 'errs' and 'ahs' wherever you can. The aim should be to maintain an uninterrupted flow of speech, without seeming too polished or unnatural.

It will do us well to remember that body language is but one communication skill which has its limitations in the amount and the range of information it can convey. It is most suited to portraying emotions and attitudes. But since it also has a vital role in supporting or contradicting verbal communication, it needs to be developed in the same way as other communication skills are developed.

Speech is the mother,
not the handmaid of thought

—Karl Krans

USING VOICE EFFECTIVELY

Adolf Hitler is reported to have once declared: 'I know that one is able to win people far more by the spoken than by the written word, and that every great movement on this globe owes its rise to the great speakers and not to the great writers.'

It is such a pity that although many years of our lives are spent in learning the skills of written communication, too few of them are dedicated to learning the art of verbal communication. Too little is known about how to speak, and especially about how to listen.

When you talk to others, certain things happen which don't happen when you hand someone a note, listen to the radio or read a newspaper. Only through speech can we relate to each other immediately and change our signals quickly.

For salespeople, the three most important requirements are health, appearance and speech. Yet, while sufficient attention is perhaps paid to health and appearance, not many are concerned about improving and perfecting 'speech'.

In India we have a long way to go before corporate managements realise that the most important item in a salesperson's kit is his voice. salesperson will go through one to four week initiation programmes with classroom sessions covering all details of company history, company policy, working rules and regulations, systems and procedures, methods of working, product details, background of research and development, and production methods. This is usually followed up with in-field training during which the new salesperson is accompanied by the sales supervisor or a senior salesperson. Then there are the refresher courses every year.

But, at every stage of this development process, the training of the voice is either forgotten or ignored. The company will have spent a few thousands on the salesperson's kit—his bag, literature folder, stationery samples or demonstration model. And they forget, as does the salesperson, that the effectiveness of all this equipment is really dependent on the salesperson's ability to make the presentation to the customer. This ability is in turn dependent on his voice range, the tone control, the facial expression and the eye contact.

We have been so tied up in the audience-oriented approach of selling that we have almost totally lost out on the speaker-oriented approach. Admittedly, the former is more important. That is what sales cybernetics is all about. But it must also be realised that some emphasis on the speaker makes the audience-oriented approach more effective.

It is time that we recognise the role of the voice in selling. The study of voice is known as paralinguistics, i.e., parallel to words. The six dimensions of paralinguistics, which add colour and flavour to the meaning of words, are volume and tone, pitch and quality, and speed (pace) and emphasis (stress). A well-trained voice can make a sale while a poor voice can mar one, all other things being equal.

VOICE AND THE AIDA FORMULA

It is the salesperson's mastery over the art of verbal communication that will make the implementation of the AIDA (Attention, Interest, Desire and Action) formula either effective or ineffective.

There are so many salesperson who are just not able to get the customer's *attention*. The initial greeting is so limp that what should have been a bright and cheery 'Good morning' sounds like a wet and grudging 'Good night'. Nothing that the salesperson does after this can revive the interview and get the customer to the next stage of *interest*.

At this point where product demonstration is the key, unless the competent salesperson modulates his voice, his gestures and his whole manner, in order to enthuse the customer, the demonstration lacks credibility and the customer cannot be transported to the *desire* stage.

At the *action* stage again, the voice and modulation, apart from the message content, can inspire confidence in the customer and persuade him to make a purchase decision and sign on the dotted line. If the manner in which questions are answered shows that the salesperson considers the sale as being inevitable, the chances of success are so much the brighter.

PROJECTING YOUR PERSONALITY THROUGH SPEECH

Clear and articulate speech patterns are an important part of your business image.

Do you know that:

- Articulate speech and appropriate voice are as important as the right business clothes or haircut.
- People listen to your voice, even before they hear what you say.
- If there is a discrepancy between what you say and how you say it, people can find it from your voice, not from your words. You can therefore negate what you say by the way you say it.

One of my clients spoke too fast, had a high pitched voice and sounded young on the phone; he diminished his authority and effectiveness, especially when talking with older clients. When he learned to lower his voice and speak slowly, his credibility soared.

Your voice may sound deep, resonant and wonderful to your ears, but do you know what you sound like to others? Tape your voice and find out, and then take appropriate action to remedy the defects. Increasing breath control will help in voice control. Take a deep breath and exhale as you count from one to five. Repeat the exercise until you can exhale while you count from one to ten.

Soft Voice

Use this when you want to give importance to what you are saying and want your listeners to focus on it. An inappropriately soft voice can be corrected by taking deep breaths and opening your mouth wider.

Pitch

A high-pitched voice can convey youth or nervousness. To find your correct pitch, start with a high pitch and lower your pitch, until you find a comfortable pitch to speak in. Having found it, keep practising to speak at this pitch until it comes to you naturally.

Pace

If you speak too fast, you may give the impression of either being nervous or hurried. Take deep breaths to slow down, and concentrate on breath control and natural pause points.

Speaking too slowly makes you sound unnatural and condescending. To correct this, put more energy into your voice and shorten your pauses.

Enunciation

Poor enunciation is usually the result of tension. This could make the speaker sound unsure, nervous or poorly educated. Yawning widely is a quick and easy way to reduce tension that affects enunciation. Exercising shoulder and neck muscles, doing neck and shoulder rolls, and saying the vowel sounds (A E I O U) several times will also help.

Confidence, authority and credibility are conveyed by a low pitch, a medium pace, a strong, resonant tone and clear enunciation.

THE ART OF ACTIVE LISTENING

Many salesperson feel that their job is to talk, talk and talk, while that of the customer is to listen, listen and listen all the time. In today's environment, before he can implement the actual selling, the salesperson has to be a good listener. In fact, if he masters the art of 'asking questions and then listening' as a normal routine, he can gather more information which can be used to sell more effectively, than rushing into an interview like a bull in a china shop.

We spend 70 per cent of our waking moments in communicating. Of this, 9 per cent is spent in writing, 16 per cent in reading, 30 per cent in talking and 45 per cent in listening. This just shows how important listening is in the communication process.

It is often said that it is not for nothing that God gave mortals two ears and only one tongue. Therefore, there must have been a purpose in this design.

Unfortunately, most salesperson are not trained to listen, in the same way as they are not trained to use their voice to maximum effect. Though both aspects are very important, both are most often ignored, and a disproportionate emphasis is laid on product knowledge, company policy and the basics of selling techniques. All this training can have less than the required effect in the marketplace because tone control and listening skills have been forgotten.

Good listening helps clients to feel good and comfortable. Only after this stage do they open up and give vent to their real objections or inner feelings. That is why the good salesperson is trained to listen with empathy, not with sympathy.

Poor listeners are identified by one of these signs—they interrupt, jump to conclusions, finish the other person's sentence, their eyes wander, their posture is poor, they change the subject, write everything down or fidget with something or the other. Watch out for these signs.

The professional salesperson is a professional at listening and he knows that the higher he goes up the organisation, the more he needs to listen.

SELLING BY LISTENING—SOCRATIC SELLING

We have now come from the 'age of selling by talking' to the 'age of selling by listening'. The salesperson is now expected to talk 40 per cent of the time and listen 60 per cent of the time, perhaps, even listen 70 per cent of the time. The trick is to ask questions and listen, and again ask questions and listen. The more you find out about the customer, the better you can tailor your sales approach to his needs and wants, rather than to what you think he should want.

A powerful way to open a sales call was inspired by Socrates, the Greek philosopher. Socratic selling is greatly different from traditional selling. 'Mr Shah, I came prepared to talk about the rapid transportation system we discussed on the telephone,' the salesperson may say. 'If you could give me your views on that, we can focus this meeting on what interests you.' The salesperson just yields the floor. The customer opens up and gives a lot of useful information. A high level of trust is established and the customer owns the decisions made.

When you adopt the Socratic approach, the call takes a whole new direction. The representative can learn more about what is going on within the customer's company than in a year of working with them. The opening lets the customer tell the salesperson what he needs. It also tells the salesperson where the call is headed. He can then tell in the first few minutes if the customer is in a 'buying' mood or in a 'get him out of here quick' mood.

When meetings begin with a Socratic opener, salespersons are amazed that a 20-minute call often turns into a two-hour session, with the customer ignoring the clock and doing most of the talking. The Socratic opener puts customers exactly where they want to be.

After all, the meetings are on their turf, taking up their time. They expect meetings to be focussed on their needs. Customers do not need a pitch; they need an opportunity to explain and to think out loud.

The Socratic beginning gives them the opportunity in a way that shows respect, assures them that the salesperson is well prepared and promises that the meeting will be shaped by their interest. It paves the way for dialogue in which the salesperson listens carefully, asks questions that help buyers think and assists buyers in making good decisions.

The Socratic method synthesises human nature with our selling objectives and lays the groundwork for proposals. The opener is just the first of a series of open-ended questions that Socratic salespeople use to uncover needs and help customers reach sound buying decisions. The Socratic dialogue is fuelled by these phrases: 'What do I need to know?' 'Why do you say that?' 'Tell me more about it?' These invitations draw out the full story and prevent salespeople from jumping to unwarranted conclusions.

The Socratic approach prevents the salespeople from succumbing to the temptation to argue and persuade in the face of objections. For all of us selling in the 21st century, Socrates is still alive and relevant.

PREPARED NOTES OR IMPROMPTU SPEECH

This is always a controversial subject. Should there be a structured selling speech committed to memory or should one play it by ear? There is no firm answer to this question. The more technical the subject, the greater the need for structured selling, e.g., selling high-value engineering items, pharmaceutical products and pesticides. The less technical the item—soap, shampoo, razor blades, etc.—the smaller the need for a structured approach.

However, all selling requires planning. If there is a plan, then one already knows the objective of the visit and, therefore, what one will say during the call. For a professional salesperson, there will seldom be an unplanned call, which means that there will always be a framework of an approach playing at the back of his mind, whether he is going to repeat it verbatim or improvise.

The more seasoned the salesperson, the less he will rely on a verbatim detailing. The newer salesperson, especially if he is selling a technical product, needs to rely on a verbatim detailing. It is better to appear unnatural and artificial with verbatim detailing, than to make major factual errors in the presentation while trying to improvise.

The ideal, of course, is to be entirely familiar with the structured presentation, but put it across so naturally that it seems impromptu. It is the technique used by stage actors who commit lines to memory, but present them in a fresh and natural manner even in the fiftieth performance of the play.

> *The secret of joy in work is contained in one word—excellence. To know how to do something well is to enjoy it.*
>
> —Pearl S. Buck

THE DRAMA OF SELLING

I had always thought that the great comedian Bob Hope cracked one joke after another and kept the audience in splits of laughter because he was witty, quick to react with repartee, could think on his feet and had the ability to see the funny side of every situation. But it was much more than that. He thought about every joke in advance. He wrote it out, rehearsed it, arranged the sequence, organised for some people from the audience to participate and had assistants in the wings of the stage on both sides who would hold up placards with the jokes written on them in large letters. There was a sequential order for placards to be set up on the left and right side of the stage, right through the show.

As a selling professional, all this had many lessons for me. For those on stage and those in selling, preparation is the foundation for success. It involves writing the script, rehearsing it, going through every movement in your mind's eye, right from the initial handshake and taking a chair, to the tone with which you will say 'Good Morning'.

For the actor and the salesperson, nothing happens by accident. There is always a plan which has been rehearsed, both mentally and physically. And yet, both on stage and in selling, the person has to appear to be natural and spontaneous. He cannot seem like a parrot, monotonously and disinterestedly repeating a script of a selling story that has been prepared for him by his head office. Both on stage and in selling, the person must bring freshness to the delivery. It does not matter whether it is the first show or the hundredth, the first interview or the hundredth. On every occasion, the salesperson must appear to be making the first presentation.

The standards to be maintained are always high, whether it is a full house or a nearly empty house. Whether the customer is warm and seems greatly interested, or cold and distant, it should not affect the salesperson. This is what distinguishes the professional actor or salesperson from the amateur. And both the actor and the salesperson improve with every show and every interview. They always aim for perfection. They try to excel in what seem minor aspects—the way they bring out the literature, handle a sample or model, or use a pointer or pen.

Sir Lawrence Olivier, the great Shakespearean actor, once said that he practised lighting a cigarette for three days, because he wanted to be perfect at lighting a cigarette on stage. Yes, actors and salesperson have a lot in common, which is why those on stage are salesperson and salesperson have to be, or seem to be, on stage.

QUESTIONS TO REFLECT ON

1. Which of the non-verbal factors in communication do you consider most important? Can you list them in order of importance?
2. What are the six dimensions of paralinguistics?
3. Are there any other questions you need to ask to study the customer?
4. Is it natural that very knowledgeable salesperson are inclined to focus less on the customer as the star? Can this be corrected?
5. Could you list some of the ways of communicating through body language, which have a common meaning globally?
6. How can you train yourself to use a planned sales talk in a natural way?

ACTION POINTS

1. List five situations where you have made the customer a star. How was this done?
2. List five situations where you missed the opportunity to do this. How did this happen?

3. Prioritise the nine dimensions of body language. Then focus on improving these over a nine-month period (one month for each).
4. Practise speaking into a tape recorder. Listen to your voice. Improve your paralinguistic skills. Do this repeatedly. It could take many months.
5. Practise the Socratic method in selling. Time yourself. Are you asking the right questions? Are you listening 60 per cent of the time. Do this at every interview over six months or longer till it comes naturally to you.

CHAPTER 7

Making the Sales Presentation

Knowledge is the asset
innovation is the process.

—Debra Arnidon

It is human to be nervous and jittery before an important sales presentation. Training for a major sales presentation involves learning how to channel nervous energy into productive energy. To do this the following techniques are important:

1. *Imagine* going through the whole process of the meeting, beginning with greeting the customer, shaking hands, etc., and the picture of the person(s) you are going to meet. You should check out what the company is like and try to picture the office and the set-up.
2. *Mentally rehearse the presentation*, your facial expressions, hand movements, etc., so that you have a clear picture of the pattern of the presentation.
3. *Visualise the objections* to your presentation and how you will deal with them. Make a list of questions most likely to be raised and rehearse your answers.
4. *Rehearse with a co-worker* who will be objective in the appraisal and will also help simulate the dialogue of a sales presentation.

You must feel confident and project it too. Be careful of a nervous voice or a poise that indicates a lack of self-confidence. Also be aware of your negative body language. Practice before the actual presentation will help you to overcome this. Remember, 'practice makes a man perfect'.

PRECONCEIVED IMPRESSIONS

Can a salesperson afford to have preconceived impressions? Can he afford to make up his mind about a customer before meeting him? The answer is 'No'. In fact, it is dangerous for a salesperson to lose his objectivity, to be guided by rumours and to form opinions based on hearsay. The professional salesperson needs to come to his own conclusions, based on his own experiences and knowledge. Prejudging can often mean lost opportunities.

JUMPING TO CONCLUSIONS

Roy, a medical representative with a pharmaceutical company, had been in the profession for just under a year. Surprisingly, he had not yet met Dr Rajan, an eminent physician in his area. He said that he tried to meet Dr Rajan several times during this period. But every time he was either not there or was too busy.

But Roy's problem went much deeper. He was reluctant to meet this customer because another salesperson had told him many months ago that Dr Rajan was a very awkward customer. He was brusque to the point of being rude, asked difficult questions about the product and appeared to enjoy the salesperson's discomfort. Roy was somewhat relieved that he had not been able to meet Dr Rajan.

Late one evening, Roy was at a chemist shop. It began raining heavily; he had no umbrella and decided to wait till the fury abated. Suddenly a car pulled up and Dr Rajan came in. He had wanted to buy some injections and had decided to stop by on the way home. Roy greeted him and introduced himself. Dr Rajan was very cordial. He collected his parcel and turned back to get into his car. Then he stopped. 'Are you here because of the heavy rain?' he asked Roy. 'Can I give you a lift somewhere? Where do you stay?' In fact, he was going that way and could drop him en route.

In the car, they had a pleasant conversation about the weather, the political situation, Roy's background and his company. When Roy got down from the car, he stood there on the road in the rain, thinking how wrong he had been about Dr Rajan. He had perhaps wasted a full year of opportunities because he had built a false image based on other people's coloured opinions.

LITTLE THINGS COUNT

Not many people realise that it is the little things that count—that distinguish the salesperson with finesse from the one who does not care, the professional salesperson from a traveller.

What are these little, insignificant clues? The salesperson's kit, his bag, briefcase or file. Are these clean? Is the bag arranged in such a way that the salesperson can pick out what he wants, without losing eye contact? Does the salesperson keep the bag on the customer's table or counter? Does he keep the bag on the opposite side from where the customer is sitting, so that the customer is not tempted to take a peek? Is the literature in good condition, and the samples fresh and clean, rather than soiled, covered with dust or dog-eared? Does the salesperson point out the relevant place with a pointer or pencil, instead of a finger? These are little things that count. A discriminating customer will make mental notes and distinguish the professional salesperson from the amateur.

There is a well-known film *The Art of Two Way Communication* in which the opening sequence shows a salesperson calling on a housewife to sell heating systems. The housewife does not want to buy and says no. But she cannot close the door because, inadvertently, the salesperson has put his foot in the doorway. The customer is annoyed. All chances of converting the 'no' to 'perhaps' or finally to 'yes' are blown up, only because the salesperson had his foot in the doorway. Little things count!

How often do we see a salesperson push back his chair and cross his legs, a posture unbecoming of a salesperson at an interview. Little things count.

Some salesperson will light a cigarette, without as much as a 'with your permission', or even while they can see a poster saying 'Thank you for not smoking.' Little things count.

Some salesperson will pick up a pencil, an ashtray or a paperweight from the customer's table and play with it, all the time oblivious of what they are doing. But the customer sees and knows. Unfortunately, little things count.

THE INITIAL IMPACT ON THE CUSTOMER

It is a strange phenomenon. It is the same with a sprint in athletics and an interview in a sales situation. Well begun is half done, and only the other half needs to be done during the rest of the interview. A good start gives you a big lead. A poor start sets you at a disadvantage from which it takes a long time to recover.

Communication between the customer and the salesperson begins much before the salesperson starts, much before the salesperson has spoken the first words. The first few minutes are the most important part of the interview. This is the time when you get the customer's full attention. Much of your market investigation, and the planning that is derived from it, is to be focussed on how you will start the interview.

In the first few minutes, the customer concentrates more than at any other time during the interview. Don't waste this great advantage. Try and capture as large a piece of this concentration as you can, with your approach and proposition. Saying, 'How are you?' or 'Good Morning' in a limp and disinterested fashion is exactly the reverse of what you should be saying. What you say in the first few minutes will decide the customer's attitude towards you, your product and your company.

Getting attention is an art; it is a skill acquired over the years with self-discipline, constant practice and a well worked out plan. You can get attention by either a question or a statement. You can get attention by either beginning with social conversation ('Did your son get admission into an engineering college? I remember you were quite concerned about this, the last time I was here.') or by getting straight into a business conversation ('I thought you should be among the first to know about this new product from Solray, Mr Shah.').

You can get attention by selling the idea behind the product rather than the product itself. It stirs the imagination of the customer and indicates how he will benefit, rather than make it quite obvious to him that you have something to sell.

There is no formula. Each salesperson will have his own style, his own approach. How he does it is not important, provided he sells himself as a salesperson. Genuineness counts. Trying to appear like someone else may get attention but not the kind one is seeking. In addition to being 'himself', the salesperson will have to be well-groomed, punctual, neat and pleasant. And then, it will be the first few words, both in content and tone, that will make the difference.

Clothes make the sale

It is said that 'the first impression is the last impression'. It does seem such a trite and common remark. Yet, how true it is! People jump to conclusions about the quality of the product and the reputation of the company based on how the salesperson looks.

The salesperson need not look like Sylvester Stallone or Jackie Shroff. What is important is that he looks well groomed. He need not dress at the height of fashion, with Benetton shirts or Park Avenue trousers. What is important is that he should be neatly and appropriately dressed.

His hair should be trimmed and combed. The look of studied carelessness is fine for artists, sculptors, musicians and actors, but not for salesperson. The salesperson must be clean shaven, or have a well-trimmed beard and moustache. His clothes must be clean, ironed and in sober colours, especially the necktie. salesperson have the temptation of sometimes using very bright colours and/or very broad/narrow ties. The collar and cuffs should not be frayed. Shoes should be polished and, irrespective of what people may say, *chappals* and sandals are certainly not acceptable.

Finger nails should be clean and trimmed as the customer is bound to notice them, especially at the demonstration stage of the interview. Teeth should be brushed and clean. Use a mouthwash, if necessary. Chewing paan and talking with a paan-filled mouth is totally unacceptable.

Very few people are conscious of body odour. Apart from being regular with baths, it may be necessary to use talcum powder or a deodorant. Summers can be a particularly trying time with the heat and the dust. Wearing pure cotton during these months will certainly help. No customer will tell you about body odour but it will certainly reflect on the sale.

All this shows consideration for the customer. You honour him by being well turned out. It does not matter if he himself is in crumpled clothes and is chewing paan. He is the customer and you do your best for him.

It is important to remember that the way you look reflects on the quality of your product or service, and the image of your company. You cannot lose out on the first and most important step. If you do, it will be very difficult to get on with the subsequent steps towards a successful close.

On a Lighter Note

An attractive lady walked into the men's section of a department store and asked the salesperson: 'What do you give a man who has everything?'

The salesperson, after thinking for a minute replied: 'Encouragement, young lady, encouragement!'

******

Customer to door-to-door salesperson: 'To what do you owe your extraordinary success ?'

Salesperson: 'To the first five words I say when a woman opens the door—"Miss, is your mother in?"'

MAKE A PROMISE AND KEEP IT

The power of innovative selling

When I asked the private transport company, operating buses from Bengaluru to the hill station of Ooty, if they could organise some accommodation for me and my family through their contacts, they gave me a card. 'My Tourist Corporation' it read. It was located close by, so I decided to go there right away.

I located the place easily. There was a big sign that said 'Hotel reservations confirmed in five minutes'. We went up and met the proprietor. He asked us what our requirement was, our budget and other details. Then he recommended a double room with an extra bed at the Ratan Tata Officers' hostel. He told us the price, asked for a token advance and handed over a confirmed reservation slip. Yes, it had taken 10 minutes instead of five. But he did not phone, cable or telex. How did he manage this?

Apparently, he booked rooms in advance in various hotels in India and underwrote the occupancy. He could then satisfy customers, both regular and occasional, like I had been. He took a risk in booking the rooms because he might not have found customers for all of them. But it is the same with stocks of garments, packaged foods or any other item. And his business increased because he had worked out a unique selling proposition. He provided customer satisfaction, at a profit to himself, in a way most other travel agents had not done.

Misdirected selling

People at the head office could never understand why Mulay could not meet the very reasonable targets for his area. He knew his products thoroughly, put forward a good appearance and inspired confidence. On nearly every call, doctors saw him gladly and listened to him attentively.

One day, I had accompanied him to the field. His company had introduced a new anti-diarrhoeal—effective and safe, with no side effects. 'There's nothing like it in the market,' he said truthfully. 'No other product has the same advantages.' He went on to speak very informatively about the various technical merits of the product. The doctor did not doubt a word of what Mulay said. He even affirmed the points Mulay was making. But there were no prescriptions! Somehow, Mulay had forgotten that his job was to sell the product benefits and, consequently, the product, not the product properties! And he lost the sale.

Cutting through the initial sales resistance

Door-to-door salesperson are normally not encouraged by residents in Mumbai. But there was one salesperson, Ramesh, who generally did not get the door shut on his face. He sold soft green brooms.

He would knock on the door politely. On opening the door, his prospective customers would face a pleasant, sincere smile and a polite voice asking: 'Do you have a good broom in the house?'

While the customer debated this mentally, he would produce one of his brooms from his neat sack and add: 'Here is a good broom for just five rupees each. Shall I give you two or will one be enough?' He closed 60 per cent of his sales calls, for he had mastered the art of getting attention.

DISTRACTIONS MUST BE CONTROLLED

During the interview there may be distractions of various kinds, disturbing the smooth flow of conversation.

There could be an interruption (telephone call or visitors), in which case you wait for the client to finish, then summarise what you said earlier and continue. Or wait for him to finish, then ask a question to connect the threads and continue.

There may be others present when you call—friends or business associates. Try to involve them in the conversation, at least with your eyes. The customer's mind may wander. Pause briefly. During the silence, he will come back to reality. Then proceed. In any case, the surest way to hold attention is to maintain eye contact. This ensures that the customer you are talking to is 'with you'.

INITIATING THE CONTACT

A casual approach in a sales meeting

Before each call, salesperson Gujral decides upon the exact sentence or thought with which he is going to start his sales conversation.

Salesperson Shah does not think this possible. He feels this should grow spontaneously out of the momentary situation; otherwise he would give the impression that the conversation was memorised. The other salespeople at the meeting have differing views.

What is your opinion?

A dramatic approach

'Mr Vora, you threw away Rs 300 by not buying our product Gala under the special discount offer', says Patil. Vora and some other customers listen to him with amusement. Others get angry. In some cases, Patil is successful.

'Well, if I don't get any attention with that, how else should I get it?' Patil asks.

What is your comment?

Is this too brief?

'How would you like to quickly sell out 50 dozen bottles of Gala Orange Juice?' salesperson Roy asks the retailer.

What is so special about this sentence, and why?

Casualty with a casual approach

Tommy is very firm in his belief about how to approach the customer. He tries to establish quick contact with some general conversation. It is his belief that this approach ensures that the customer is relaxed, free from any feeling of a 'special event' that might make him too cautious. He usually starts with the words, 'I happened to be passing by, so I just thought I'd drop in.' The customer takes him just as casually.

> *Knowledge is a process of piling up facts*
> *wisdom lies in their simplification.*
>
> —Martin Fischer

DEMONSTRATION—KEY TO SUCCESSFUL SELLING

Customers want to see and hear, preferably also touch, smell and feel. The more senses one involves, the more the chances of remembering. After all, you want the customer to remember your product, and then, hopefully, to buy it. Therefore, it always pays to demonstrate whatever you may sell. Even insurance can be demonstrated by working out the calculations to show how the customer will benefit.

The voice, mannerisms and attitude should lend credence to the demonstration and add force to it. Printed matter should be used with the aplomb of a professional—taken out of the bag smoothly, kept one foot away from the customer and at a slant, synchronising the spoken word with what is being shown and using a pointer instead of a finger. All this should help the customer to draw the right conclusion from the demonstration, a conclusion that you intended him to draw.

If possible, you should show your product in use—the kitchen mixer in action, the motorcar and the bicycle in motion. It is even better to involve the customer in the demonstration. Some products lend themselves to being demonstrated with a dramatic touch. This helps considerably.

Ride and try—take the keys

When I went to buy a bicycle for my son Samir, the salesperson at the shop showed me the different models available. Low seat or high seat, gears or no gears, and so on. When he saw a spark of interest in Samir's eyes, he got a lead and concentrated on just two models. He pulled these out and encouraged Samir to ride these down the road. The salesperson gave the customer a feeling of possession. He got the customer involved.

Seeing is believing

You can't help noticing him near Victoria Terminus station in Mumbai. Most times you notice him with a start, because in a flash of movement, he jerks a pen and sprinkles some blobs of ink on his shirtsleeve. In another smooth movement, he dips some cotton wool into a bottle of ink remover and cleans up the ugly ink blobs on the clean white shirt. Nothing much is said. But onlookers and passers-by don't need any more information. Many buy the ink remover, thinking of their school-going kids at home and the mess they make with ink pens. The power of demonstration!

Banerji's approach

Salesperson Banerji has some exceptionally good sales material at his disposal: tests, statistical information, letters of recommendation, illustrations and wall posters, all put nicely in order, in a brown envelope given to him by the company. He does not bring this out at an interview because he does not like to give others an impression that he is only a 'salesperson'.

At the end of the interview, however, he hands over the envelope containing all the literature to the customer with the request that he may go through this at his leisure.

What do you think of this approach?

Measured by success

Salesperson Vora was not particularly bright, his appearance inelegant, his speech caustic, his mannerisms irritating. On the other hand, salesperson Gupta was smart, well-educated and well-mannered.

Vora always took out his catalogue at the beginning of his call and showed the pictures and details of his products. Even if the customer said that he knew it all (which happened at almost every visit), he was not confused and just went on with his demonstration. As a result, he brought back a series of orders. On the other hand, Gupta thought this method undignified.

Why do you think Vora got more sales than Gupta? What is it that made the difference?

The mirror trick

There are two of them on the pavement at Flora Fountain in Mumbai. A range of sunglasses are laid out on a white cloth. The target customers are office-goers in the area, who have a quick lunch and then take a walk down the heart of Mumbai's business centre.

Raj and Shyam have the same range of products, at the same price. But Shyam does at least twice as much business as Raj. When a passer-by stops, picks up a pair and tries it on, Shyam immediately holds up a mirror in front of him, and softly exclaims, 'Looks good on you, Sir.'

The power of demonstration! Many interested observers get converted into customers.

> *On a Lighter Note*
>
> Salesperson demonstrating a sofa: 'Another good feature about it is that when guests arrive unexpectedly, it cannot be turned into a bed!'

PERSONALISED SELLING

Each salesperson at every selling interview faces the very difficult and delicate task of creating a desire to buy. He must be able to appeal both to the mind and the heart. He must be able to convert a need into a desire, or work it the other way round and show the desire to be a need.

Even while selling industrial products, the salesperson has to appeal to the heart, and not stop after presenting a series of logical arguments, which only appeal to the mind. The salesperson should never forget that the purse is closer to the heart than the mind. All things being equal, the customer will buy from a salesperson whom he likes and trusts.

It is generally found that the more qualified the salesperson, the less he focuses on the heart. He feels that the technical knowledge which he has is sufficient to carry him through with a sale. The hawker on a train or a pavement has no such pretensions. He relies heavily on 'heart' selling and not just 'hard' selling. And in this process he converts the desire into a need, or converts the need into desire.

For the salesperson, this is a constant challenge because customers are often caught between the two conflicting forces of need and desire.

The need may be to have the house repaired. The desire may be to buy a colour TV set. What will he finally buy? To an extent, it depends on the circumstances, as also on the ability of a salesperson to channel these conflicting forces into the same direction—culminating in not only a sale for the salesperson, but also in satisfaction for the customer.

The customer must like and want to have what is offered. You can only do this if you aim at the wants and needs of the customer. The customer is not an average person; he is special and different from every other person in the world.

This makes it necessary to adopt what is called *personalised selling*. It calls for the salesperson to do his homework on the prospective customer's profile in advance; to tailor his selling story to the customer's background, temperament, needs, attitudes, opinions and beliefs; to follow up on calls; and, finally, to make the customer feel that he is the only one.

Follow these norms

- Make sure you are there 10 minutes before time.
- Leave sufficient time for travel, especially if you are working in a crowded city like Mumbai or a city with poor public transportation like Bengaluru.
- Always knock before entering.
- Never sit down until you are offered a seat.
- Do not extend your hand to women customers unless they make the first move.
- Never smoke while waiting or during the interview, even if there is no 'No Smoking' sign.
- Smile and bring joy and liveliness to the presentation.
- Use your voice effectively.
- Tailor your approach and presentation to this customer.
- Enter with a prepared presentation, but be capable of a quick change if circumstances change (change in person expected to be seen, change in the mood of the customer, etc.).

Remember

- The 21st century professional salesperson is 30 per cent thinker and 70 per cent doer.

- He spends 40 per cent of interview time talking and 60 per cent of the interview time listening.
- He tries to spend 60–70 per cent time face-to-face with the customer and 30–40 per cent time travelling and waiting.

Selling is Serving in this Bookshop

Strand is a well-known bookshop in the business district of Mumbai. It is not very large. In fact there are much larger bookshops in the city. Yet it is very popular. State ministers, trade unionists, lawyers, professors and students are seen here, browsing through, spending hours in silence and in the happy company of books.

The owner sits in a corner. No one hovers around you to ask if they can help you or what you are looking for. You can spend an hour and walk out without buying anything at all. Or you can ask the knowledgeable proprietor for information on other books you may be looking for. He will get a book for you from overseas, or will give you books on approval or even tell you which other shop you could get the book from.

What is the secret of his success? It is his genuine interest in the needs of people and in people themselves. For him, selling is serving. He is there to help a customer. And with this attitude, he cannot help but make it a constantly growing group of customers.

Selling to the heart

Salesperson Ram reports: 'I proved all the advantages of the product to the customer. He recognised and accepted them all. He also agreed that our special offer was favourable. He had the money to spend. And yet, he showed no readiness to buy. I cannot understand it.' Can you?

The selling approach in the unlikeliest of places

Ramu is an urchin in rags who travels in the Minar Express which goes from Mumbai to Hyderabad. He is without a ticket and has no business to be on the train. He is there, like many others, to eke out a living by begging. But he has gone off on a different track. He cleans the whole compartment with a rag, and then comes around asking for dole. The compartment is normally quite dirty, with passengers littering the place and the railway service being poor at maintenance. Ramu, in fact, provides a significant service. And many passengers give willingly because Ramu provides a needed service.

> ### *On a Lighter Note*
>
> Pamela: 'Mummy, what becomes of a car, when it gets too old to run anymore?'
> Mummy: 'Why my girl! Someone sells it to your father as a second car, a great used car, as good as new.'
>
> ******
>
> Customer: 'I've come to buy that car you showed me yesterday.'
> Salesperson: 'That's fine. Tell me, which major feature made you decide to buy this car?'
> Customer: 'My wife.'

QUESTIONS TO REFLECT ON

1. Is there anything else you would like to add to in the preparation for a presentation?
2. What other 'little things' can you add that have contributed to 'loss of sale'?
3. Why are the first few minutes of the interview so important? Are they more important than any other stage of the interview? Is the stage of creating attention as important in creative selling as it is in attending selling?
4. Can you think of any other distractions that can disrupt an interview? How will you deal with such distractions?
5. What are the 'opening phrases' that you generally use and have found to be effective?
6. Is there any merit in having a packaged and prepared introduction to the interview? Will it seem artificial and stilted? What are the advantages of improvisation?
7. Can you list 10 examples of how salesperson have used the power of demonstration to 'clinch' the sale?
8. Can you give three examples each of where need is converted to desire and desire to need?

9. What is the connection between the 'special person' who must desire your product and 'mass-customisation' as a concept?

ACTION POINTS

1. Organise customer/salesperson mock sessions with your colleagues. Try to do this every fortnight for two hours.
2. Compare the contents of your sales kit with the sales kits of three other colleagues. Find out what is missing. Correct the situation.
3. Frame about five 'start sentences' for different kinds of customers. Test these out in the field. Amend as necessary.
4. List out examples where salesperson have successfully used:
   Dramatic touch
   Involvement of customers
   Brochures/samples
5. Identify two salesperson who are well dressed. List the reasons for why they stand out.
6. Identify five situations where 'innovative selling' is used. How and why are these situations and approaches different?

CHAPTER 8

Objections—When the Customer Says 'No'

Some of the best lessons we ever learn, we learn from our mistakes and failures. The error of the past is the wisdom and success of the future.

—Tryon Edwards

Sales trainers will keep repeating that objections from customers show that the customer is really interested in your proposition. Books on selling keep quoting the slogan 'Selling only begins when the customer says no'. Films on selling will keep motivating us to deal with objections.

Yet, when a customer does raise an objection, most of us resent it. We feel hurt. We take it as a personal attack, an affront. The customer is seen to be against the salesperson, against his company and against his product. This attitude towards the customer's objection is reflected in the salesperson's eyes, his expression, his whole body posture and his language. The eyes glint with disappointment, the expression hardens and the smile vanishes, the body posture stiffens and the language becomes defensive, sometimes even defiant.

In this process the empathy between the customer and the salesperson is lost. The bond of camaraderie or fellowship that has been so carefully built through this interview, and previous ones, is snapped. That is why it is so important to not just know the answers to commonly raised objections, but also develop the right attitude to objections—to really believe and feel

- that the raising of an objection is a good thing for the customer, the selling process and the salesperson;
- that through these objections he is making progress and getting somewhere;
- that this objection is directed at the product and not at the salesperson, thereby isolating one from the other;
- that any customer has the right to clarify and raise objections before he spends his money; and
- that the salesperson, in the role of a customer, would do exactly the same thing.

If this attitude is developed by the salesperson over a period of time, he graduates into being a truly professional salesperson. He welcomes and, in fact, enjoys situations where customers raise objections and ask questions. In cricket the more difficult the ball, the greater the challenge the batsman feels in responding to it. And greater still is the victory he enjoys in smashing it to the boundary. Such is the stuff great salespersons are made of. Many years of discipline temper them and distinguish them from just ordinary salespersons.

ATTITUDE TO OBJECTIONS

How do you view objections? Do they irritate and annoy you as unnecessary time-wasters which prevent you from closing the sale? Have you ever thought of them as 'doubts' in the customer's mind that he would like to clarify?

An informal survey was done to find out how salespeople reacted to objections. It was found that

- 44 per cent gave up after receiving the first objection;
- 22 per cent gave up after receiving the second objection;
- 16 per cent gave up after receiving the third objection;
- 10 per cent gave up after receiving the fourth objection.

This left only 8 per cent of salespeople to still sell! The survey also showed that 73 per cent of the customers voiced five or more objections, before placing an order.

OBJECTIONS SHOULD BE WELCOMED

Many salesperson walk out of an interview very happy that the customer has given them a patient hearing, nodded all the time and not raised any controversial issues.

In fact, this is really a poor interview. It only shows that the customer has not been stimulated, has not asked questions and, therefore, will perhaps not buy. It is rightly said that 'it is dangerous not to have any objections'. It is also rightly said that 'every person (salesperson) can train himself to deal with objections'.

Your company and your products are bound to have some disadvantages vis-à-vis the competition. The product that becomes the market leader is the one with the advantages highlighted successfully and the disadvantages de-emphasised.

When one really thinks about it, a product seldom has more than six possible objections. Customers may put the objection across in different ways, in different words. But the essence is usually the same—objections related to quality, price, delivery, packaging, promotion or discount.

Once the salesperson sits down and analyses the genesis of the basic objections, then he can be prepared with the answers. These answers can be developed

- with help and advice of his sales manager;
- from the experiences of his salesperson colleagues who have had similar problems and have successfully found solutions; and
- from his own experiences after testing out various answers in the field and then narrowing down on answers which work.

It is possible that one answer works with one kind of customer, while another works with another kind. These factors should be taken into account when training oneself to deal with objections.

On a Lighter Note

'How do I handle customers who compare our price today with the low prices of what they call the good old days?' a salesperson asked his boss.

'Be astonished,' the boss replied, 'and say, "I didn't think you were old enough to remember those days".'

Some Ready Answers

The kind of answers you give will obviously depend on the kind of objections raised.

- It may be an *unspoken objection*. The customer just nods his head and is totally uncommunicative.

  Ask questions. Let him talk. Draw him out.

- It may be an *excuse*, not a real objection.

  This cannot be answered. Just sidestep, ignore and proceed with the selling speech.

- It may be a *prejudice*, totally irrational and irrelevant.

  This is difficult to handle, except on an emotional plane, because it gives his ego a boost.

- It may be a *malicious objection*. This may be due to something that has hurt him in the past and about which you may not know much.

  Ignore this. Don't feel offended. Don't try to answer because there are no answers. Like in the case of excuses, sidestep and proceed with your selling.

- It may be an *objection on grounds of prestige*. This customer needs ego satisfaction. He has to be made to feel important.

  Ask for his advice and information. Make him feel he is the greatest.

- It may be a *highly individual objection*—a subjective objection. He feels that very few others have similar problems. His problems are special. This is a genuine feeling. It is not prestige issue or a malicious objection.

  This requires that you put your selling on a personal plane after studying a detailed profile of the customer. You have to detail examples of people with similar problems so that it inspires confidence.

- It may be an *objective objection*—a very rational objection, focussed on a fact, not mere feeling, and pertaining to the product.

You can build the answer into your selling presentation so that you answer it before it is raised.

- It may be a *general resistance to buying*—an attitude rather than a specific resistance.

  This requires an initial breakthrough to get the attention of the customer. Unless this breakthrough is achieved, everything else said and done later is futile.

- It may be the *last minute hurdle*. The customer says, 'Seems good, let me think and get back to you tomorrow', but he never will.

  This requires a final push by the salesperson. He must tell the customer that he is making the right decision and will not regret it. If this 'push' is not provided, the customer 'escapes'. And the order which is within reach today, slips through your fingers.

He answered all objections

Salesperson Sivaswamy knew his products very well. What is more, he knew his competitor's products as well. In the marketplace, there was tremendous respect for Sivaswamy as a professional and as an authority in his field. However, he was so imbued with the idea of answering every objection that he jumped on every excuse given by the customer for not buying, and treated it as a bona fide objection. This would go on until the time factor ended his interview. His interviews thus became ping-pong affairs.

Could Sivaswamy have handled these objections any other way?

Overcoming objections

V. M. Ranga, a well-known millionaire builder in Chennai, sat back in his chair, looking slightly distastefully at A. S. M. Virmani of Alco. When Virmani had entered Ranga's room, a buyer who was already there had been smoking. Virmani had also pulled out a cigarette after asking Ranga's permission to smoke. Ranga was busy with a series of long distance calls, so Virmani had continued to smoke. Perhaps Ranga was not too pleased about this non-stop smoking in his room.

When Ranga had finished, Virmani began his selling story about Alco. Ranga was a big potential customer and in fact bought 25 per cent of his requirement from Alco. The balance was purchased from Balco and Nalco.

Virmani asked if there were any complaints about Alco. 'Yes, the price is Rs 200 more than that of other brands,' said Ranga. Virmani interjected to say that Alco was superior in quality. 'That may be so,' Ranga said, 'but neither I nor my project people can perceive this superiority. So we really do not know why we pay more.'

Virmani seemed to be at a loss to give some explanation, except to say that Alco laboratory tests had shown that Alco was, in fact, superior. Ranga, already a little unhappy with Virmani, was obviously in no mood to accept this.

No one can make you feel
inferior without your consent.

—Eleanor Roosevelt

DEALING WITH OBJECTIONS

There is an optimum time to deal with objections. These can be handled in various ways:

- *Before* the objection is raised, as in the case of objective objections or, sometimes, subjective objections.
- *Immediately after* it is raised, as in prejudices or objections on grounds of prestige or subjective objections. This should be done rarely, and only when you cannot proceed with your talk till you have responded to the objection.
- *Long after* the objection is raised, as in desire for information. This should be done most often. It gives you a chance to reduce the weight of the objection as you keep talking. Or the objection might disappear altogether. You don't have to contradict the customer right at the beginning and therefore spoil the interview. And you don't have to break up your selling story by answering a stray objection somewhere in-between.
- *Some* objections *may never* be answered. They may be irrelevant to the discussion, as in the case of excuses, malicious objections or resistance to buy.

> *On a Lighter Note*
>
> 'Your price is too high. I can do better,' said the prospect. Salesperson: 'I don't doubt that. There's always somebody who will come back with a lower price. Let me give you an example: A friend of mine needed an operation and asked his doctor how much it would cost. The surgeon quoted Rs 3000. My friend said, "You will have to do better than that. I've got a much lower price from the undertaker."'

The style and manner of dealing with objections

Every salesperson must try to find the real objection, to penetrate the screen. Most customers are not open and forthcoming. They need probing. Only when one gets to the real objection can one solve the problem. It is important that the salesperson keep his cool even in the face of provocation. Maintaining one's composure is half the battle won.

The salesperson must be civil and respectful. It takes two to have an argument, leading to frayed tempers, uncivil language or even fisticuffs. The salesperson must be a good listener. Let the customer say all that he wants to say. Don't interrupt, hasten to answer, defend or make tall claims ('In my company, this can never happen.'). When the customer has had his say, the salesperson should ask relevant questions and get the answers.

When he has answered the customer's objection, he must move on. Not belabour the point, but move on. He should always be progressive and brief, without being curt. He should be modest and not gloat with 'You see? I was right and you were wrong.' By doing this, he may win the battle but will lose the war.

The first prerequisite is that he should know his product, his customer and his competition. Only then can he master the art of overcoming objections. Then the customer will respect him and his company and perhaps buy his products.

> *On a Lighter Note*
>
> Salesgirl to customer in a dress shop: 'But Madam, looking ridiculous is the fashion this year.'
>
> ******

(Continued)

(Continued)

> 'What do I need an encyclopaedia for?' Randhir asked the door-to-door salesperson. 'I'm well informed about everything.'
>
> 'That's just it,' pointed the salesperson. 'Just imagine all the fun you're going to have, finding all the errors they've made in it.'
>
> ******
>
> Demanding housewife: 'Are those eggs strictly fresh?'
> Grocer to assistant: 'Feel those eggs, Raj, and see if they are cool enough to sell yet.'

THANK YOUR COMPLAINING CUSTOMER—TODAY

Have you ever looked positively at a complaining customer? Have you ever thought that the complaining customer is

- telling your company that it still has a chance to keep his business;
- representing other dissatisfied customers who do not bother to complain and are probably doing more damage by word of mouth;
- informing your company about products or services that do not work, outdated features, incorrect invoices and other problems that exist within your organisation; and
- actually helping your business prosper?

RECTIFYING SERVICE MISTAKES

Things are bound to go wrong in a company. Strains can also occur in a company's relationship with its customers. The true test of a company's commitment to service is not in the pledge in its marketing literature, but in the way the company responds when things go wrong for the customer.

Customers' expectations

Customers have the following expectations from a company when things go wrong:

- *To receive an apology for the fact that the customer is inconvenienced.* When we make mistakes, many of us find it difficult, first of all, to admit that we have made a mistake and, second, to say 'I'm sorry'. So if a customer has been inconvenienced in any way, let us not hesitate to apologise to him, verbally or in writing, on behalf of our company.

- *To be offered a 'fair compensation' for the problem.* Somehow 'fairness' comes very strongly into the picture. For instance, if M/s Computer Centre has an annual maintenance contract with an organisation as per certain terms and conditions, and if these are not fulfilled by the company, the customer feels a 'sense of injustice' because he has paid in advance according to a contract, the terms of which the company has now no intention of keeping.

  Sometimes, there could be a genuine problem, beyond the control of the company, in which case the customer can be contacted and offered an explanation, displaying your sensitivity and concern. The customer will in all likelihood understand your problem.
- *To be treated in a way that suggests the company cares (a) about the problem, (b) about solving it and (c) about the customer's inconvenience.* Customers, being human, do not expect 'perfect service' but they do expect you to be concerned about their problem and rectify it quickly. So do listen to what they have to say, and try and involve them in finding a suitable solution acceptable to both.
- *To be offered some value-added atonement for the inconvenience.* One does not have to do this all the time, but it is a gesture that says, 'I'm sorry for the inconvenience caused and would like to make it up to you in some way.' Sometimes even a note may be enough.
- *That you keep your promises.* And abide by the terms of your contract, verbal or written. Show your customer that you have integrity and that you will stick by your word. Customers do not like to be lied to; they would prefer to hear the bad news just as it is, instead of being told lies.

Remember that only 4–10 per cent of the dissatisfied customers give us a chance to make things right; the rest don't bother to complain to us, but they tell everybody else!

IS THE CUSTOMER ALWAYS RIGHT?

At times, the salesperson is caught in the middle, between the customer and the company. He has to represent his company's case to the customer and the customer's case to the company. And this is to be done in a way that is fair to both, so that neither feels betrayed.

How then does the salesperson deal with the belief that 'the customer is always right?'

Some companies solve this by having a separate division to handle customer complaints. Other companies allow their salespeople to honour all claims, except fraudulent ones, and see that the customer is satisfied. However, this does not always solve the problem completely. Most knowledgeable salesperson know that there is also a painful sound to the oft repeated 'the customer is always right'. These salesperson know that customers are sometimes wrong. They hate to be in a situation where they have to submissively face a customer and say that he is right even when they well know that he is wrong. But the question is, should they do this?

Perhaps, in their own interest as salesperson, they often should. Because they must remember that selling begins when the customer says 'no'. Complaints can open up many immediate and future chances for sales.

There are salesperson who get fed up every once in a while, in their long selling career, and squarely face a complaining customer to prove that he is wrong, wrong, wrong! They are acting on a natural impulse. But the salesperson who acts on it too often wrecks himself and his company.

Allowing the customer to be right

When do we let the customer be right? Two questions could help us decide this.

1. What do we do about the complaint?
2. Is it worthwhile to let this customer be right?

Though the question is placed second, it is important to first decide if it is worth the company's while to let this customer be right.

For instance, if the customer is a big buyer and his claim represents only a fraction of his year's purchases, it would be in the company's interest to honour his claim.

If the claimant is a big new account, and the company has invested a lot of time, attention and money to make him a customer, but he has misused the unfamiliar article he bought, what would you do? If you reject his complaint, then as far as he is concerned, your goods and your company are no good. But if you adjust the claim, help him to use the article correctly and understand how it can be used best, you have probably gained a customer for life.

Strangely enough, one makes customers for life not by serving them well in good times but by serving them well in bad times. So in the long run, generosity in settling claims and letting the customer be right pays. (This of course does not refer to unreasonable or fraudulent claims.) People feel good when the company has been generous to them, and will tell others about their happy experience.

Body language signals

Body language, or non-verbal communication, is a new science. There are 70,000 body language signals, 15,000 of which are facial signals alone. It is not possible for us to control all these signals, but if there is any variance between what we are saying and our body language, the latter is correct.

Non-verbal communication from your customer/prospect can therefore tell you how you are doing. It can tell you whether you are headed for a sale, or objections and then a refusal.

So you need to be on the lookout for signals right from the start of the interview. If the signals are positive and encouraging, you can go on with your planned selling speech. If the signals are negative, then you need to change gears and deviate so that you do not get a final 'no' at the end of the interview. You need to take remedial measures in time. If you wait too long, you will finally fail.

The following are some aspects of body language that usually indicate a favourable reaction to you and your proposition:

- Nodding the head frequently
- Smiling
- Hands and arms being open and relaxed
- Leaning back to listen
- Handling literature
- Making frequent eye contact

- Tilting the head to one side
- Stroking the chin
- Legs being uncrossed
- Leaning forward to speak

All these positive signals have to be reconfirmed by asking test questions from time to time and getting agreeable answers.

If all this happens in a sales interview, the professional salesperson is well on his way to success and achievement. The closing of the sale will be natural, unforced and favourable.

QUESTIONS TO REFLECT ON

1. What is the single most important reason why salesperson resist an objection?
2. Can excuses, desire for information and the last effort to resist buying be truly classified as objections?
3. What percentage of objections, in your experience, is never required to be answered?
4. Will there be any product or service where no objections are raised?
5. Will customers not be aware when the salesperson purposely allows the customer to be right, when he is actually wrong?

ACTION POINTS

1. Make a list of all the products you sell.
2. For each product write out the features, the advantages of these features and the benefits that accrue.

   Never dwell long on features, which is what salesperson normally tend to do. Always give the benefits first, and explain 'why' by listing features only if necessary.
3. Find out three major competitors for each of your products. List the benefits of your product against those of the competitor. Do a comparative analysis. Master this information.

   When selling, highlight the benefits of your product that matter, against the bestselling competitor in that area. Do not mention competitors by name, unless forced to. Otherwise, only forcefully highlight the benefits of your product and subtly imply the disadvantages of your competitior's.

4. List all the objections to your products, classify them and work out at least two or three answers for each of them.
5. List out the objections that you will answer before, immediately and long after they are raised, or not at all. Test these in the field.
6. List the negative body signals that a salesperson must watch out for, to make sure he changes track and gets the customer interested. Avoid these signals.

CHAPTER 9

The Close and Thereafter

Always bear in mind
that your own resolution to succeed
is more important than any other one thing.
—Abraham Lincoln

The close can happen at any time and at any point in the sales conversation. It is like a shaft of light—something hits the consumer's mind, he sees a benefit and the satisfaction he will derive from the product/service, and he buys it.

There are many such points during an interview. These are the high interest points. The salesperson must identify these and close the sale at one such point. If he misses one, then he must wait for the next high point but never close at a low interest point. This can be fatal.

The salesperson must also close as fast as possible. The order that is within reach today might be beyond the mountains tomorrow. In fact, it is said that a good salesperson should start closing right from the beginning of the interview.

There are many ways in which the closing of an interview can be approached. It depends on the situation.

The salesperson can make the closing easier by getting the customer to agree to his proposition part by part. Then it is easier for the customer to agree to the final proposition of buying the product. Or he can give alternative offers. 'Would you like to take two dozen or will one dozen be enough?' Maybe he can use the concentration method, where he summarises all the advantages that chiefly interest the customer and get the customer's attention totally focussed, thus making him want to buy.

Many salesperson who have mastered most aspects of selling are still poor when it comes to closing. They are like footballers who take the ball right across the field but hesitate in front of an open goal. Since they don't ask for an order, they don't get one. They miss the opportunities. Perhaps it is because these salesperson have not trained themselves or they have not been trained to

- look for signs like facial expressions and those of speech;
- analyse significant questions like delivery time, discount on bulk quantities and special concessions;
- analyse special requests, for example, a request for a few days trial on approval;
- ask check questions that will give pointers to the customer's thinking process.

The salesperson must consider the sale as an assured event and hence exude confidence right through the interview. There is no need to give an ultimatum to the customer. But there is always a need to issue a direct or indirect invitation, without the fear of getting 'no' for an answer.

In any case, a real salesperson is never insulted by a refusal. He believes that the customer has every right to say 'no', the same way as the salesperson himself has when he is a customer. But he never gives up. And he does not write off a customer just because he did not become a customer on one particular selling interview.

A WAR OF NERVES

John had started out in selling with a lot of enthusiasm. He had said that what attracted him most to selling was the sense of challenge. But he quit in just four months and took up a desk job in a bank. What went wrong?

'Whenever I take out my order book, I can sense that the customer is nervous. As a result, I also lose my nerve. I just can't get around to asking for an order, because I know that he will say "No".' John was a good starter and a poor closer. Instead of trying to correct and improve, he chose to quit!

HOW WELL DO YOU HANDLE REJECTION

'He won't see you.'
'We are happy with our current supplier.'

'Sorry, your price is too high, we cannot afford it.'
'Sorry, I know this is the fifth time you are calling and I promised I'd see you, but something urgent has cropped up.'

How often have we heard these words that have caused us hurt, or anger, or frustration, and sometimes all three! Goldmann, in his book *How to Win Customers,* says that the salesperson's personality is under a pressure that most people can't take. He must feel at ease, cordial and friendly in the presence of people who have little or no wish to see him, or to listen to him. In the face of their resistance he has to make them aware of needs that they did not realise they had and on which they may not want to spend money. He must be tactful and agreeable.

One of the first things to remember when you get a rejection is that the customer is saying 'no' to your product or service, and not to 'you'. How often have you said 'no' to the door-to-door salesperson trying to sell your family an economical phenyl or bathroom deodorant? Why did you say 'no'? Because from your point of view, you did not need or want to buy the product. Rejecting someone's proposal is therefore natural.

So, when customers say 'no' it is because they believe that what you are suggesting is not in their best interest. However, handling rejection is like a sport. When you first start, it may be a little difficult, but as you play more often, it becomes easier. Over the years you keep trying and sharpening your skills, ultimately overcoming your fear of rejection. You find yourself suggesting options to the client that you would have never dared to do earlier.

Can one eliminate rejection from a sales career? No, but you can learn to deal with it more effectively. The following all tips for handling rejections:

- Don't be surprised when it happens. (Encountering rejection is proof that you are working.)
- Know that it is probably not you who is being rejected.
- Try to determine the reason for the rejection. Ask questions and find out why— the payment terms or the delivery schedule may be the problem, which could perhaps be sorted out.
- Try to learn something from the rejection. Have you done your best? Did you try every avenue open to you? What did you do

wrong? Can you see that as far as possible, such a thing does not happen again?

- Don't just quit after a rejection—try to get something from the prospect. Ask for another appointment, leave some literature or offer to send some additional material.
- If everything else fails, forget the prospect. In some industries you may be rejected many times before you finally get an order. However, this doesn't happen all the time. If, after real effort, you cannot change the situation you would probably be wise to give the prospect to someone else.

On a Lighter Note

One day, Ajit, a salesperson, tried out the 'alternative choice' closing technique on his sales manager.

'How much of a raise in salary will you give me—Rs 500 or Rs 300?'

The sales manager was quick to respond: 'Which do you prefer—to resign or to be fired?'

QUESTIONS TO REFLECT ON

1. Why is a salesperson diffident to ask for an order?
2. Does an order naturally follow from the AIDA sequence without further prompting? Why?
3. Are there any other ways of closing a sale?
4. What other leads do you get to indicate that the customer is ready to buy?
5. In your experience, what percentages of customers have to be completely written off?
6. Does ability to take no for an answer mean that you are thick-skinned?

ACTION POINTS

1. Close the interview at the high point of desire. You know how to identify this.

2. Show confidence in your proposition. Consider the sale as an assured event.
3. Follow all the guidelines given for closing—be brief, to the point and pleasant.
4. Do not run away after getting the order, but also do not stay too long.
5. Focus on the product that sparked the desire. Also, focus on its benefits.

CHAPTER 10

Compulsions and Reflections

ALWAYS BE AVAILABLE TO THE CUSTOMER

An authority on sales techniques likes to remind salesperson, over and over again, of a simple slogan he coined—'Be There'. This is nothing new. Salesperson have always known that they must be available to the customer at regular and frequent intervals, to make sure that he

- knows about your product;
- remembers your product;
- knows where he can get it; and
- can get it when he wants it.

You may have an excellent product, perhaps the best in the country, but if the customer does not know about it, then all the time, effort and money spent in developing it is of no use. The salesperson is needed to inform the customer about the product.

If there is a sudden epidemic of eye infections, the demand of antibiotic applicaps would immediately go up manifold. If you are marketing such a product you have to respond immediately with promotion and distribution. Or, a big cement plant is going to be set up by a corporation. If you are a supplier of cement manufacturing machinery, the earlier you get to the 'deciders', the better your chances of getting this sizeable business.

Be There

My wife had an offer to buy an imported Japanese-make washing machine. It was an excellent machine. But she was concerned about servicing, replacement parts and the warranty. There was no backup. She preferred another machine of an Indian manufacturer where she could be sure of help when there was trouble. In effect, she was looking for a salesperson who would *be there.*

That is why a salesperson must be in constant touch with his customers, not because the company says so, not because the tour programme has been laid down and not because it is a command, but because the customer wants this assurance all the time, for all types of products or services. He is looking for a company and a salesperson who will *be there.*

FRIENDSHIP WITH CUSTOMERS—A DOUBLE-EDGED SWORD

There is a well-known old saying—'Familiarity breeds contempt'. Perhaps this is not entirely true. But what is generally true is that familiarity spawns carelessness. The better we know a person, the more we are inclined to take the person for granted. It happens within our families, where a child forgets to say 'Thank you' or 'Sorry' to a parent because the parent is taken for granted. It happens between husband and wife, and it happens among brothers and sisters.

Those of us who have been in the selling profession for many years know that the same human failing also applies to salesperson in relation to their customers. With an association of many years, a good salesperson also becomes a close friend of many of his customers. It becomes a relationship that goes well beyond the call of duty. The salesperson may get involved in the school admission of the customer's son, in the marriage arrangements of his daughter or in trying to get drugs from abroad for his sick wife. The salesperson becomes a friend— this is a good thing, a healthy development.

But friendship, like many good things, is a double-edged sword. It can be a help and it can be an obstacle. The customer can take the sales-person for granted. When the salesperson makes a business call, the customer talks about his own family, asks about the salesperson's family, discusses the political situation or common friends, and then realises that he has spent a lot of time and needs to get back to business. There is an abrupt ending, with the salesperson not having got a chance to talk about his product or service. The customer of course assures the salesperson of continued help and support. There is no problem. After all, anything for a friend!

The salesperson on his part feels that he has had a very nice interview—very friendly, warm and cordial, quite unlike a typical salesperson–customer relationship. It is much beyond that and as salesperson in India are fond of saying 'The customer is in my pocket!' He may or may not be. But the sales figures often do not reflect this. Many times the sales support is in 'inverse proportion' to the extent of friendly relations between the customer and the salesperson.

The salesperson has not mastered the art of moving smoothly from social conversation to business discussion. He does not get a chance to talk about the benefits of his product, the product value and price relationship, its superiority over competition and the new improvements. The customer has forgotten all this a long time ago. A competitor who makes a purely business call talks about all these aspects. The customer gets convinced, and a sale is made by the salesperson who has the advantage of being less friendly with the customer.

There is, therefore, a great need for salesperson, especially senior and experienced salesperson, to avoid the 'friendship trap'. A customer must remain a customer first and a friend later. The moment the relationship changes, it may become friend first and customer never!

SELLING TO AN INCREASING NUMBER OF WOMEN PROSPECTS

Do you find that more and more prospects are women? Have you ever wondered why you are sometimes unable to close a sale quickly when a woman is involved in the purchasing decision? It often takes two visits or more before success is achieved. Research shows that women need to be handled differently from men. Consider the following tips for selling to women:

1. Women *dislike being interrupted frequently* when they are speaking. They perceive this as a lack of respect. Always allow the buyer to finish her comments, acknowledge them and then respond.
2. Do not view objections as challenges. Women *provide objections as points of discussion* and a way to express feelings. Men respond to objections as challenges to conquer. Do not challenge

women's objections. Find out why they were raised and identify the feelings, emotions and reasons for the objections.

3. Avoid boasting. Women *resent boastfulness* and view boastful claims as demeaning to their ability to make a proper decision. Comparisons work better than outright claims. These allow the buyer to make her own decision after seeing the facts (as when comparisons are presented in writing).
4. Maintain *eye contact.* Men perceive eye contact with other men as a confrontation and with women as showing familiarity or intimacy. Women perceive lack of eye contact by men as their lack of interest, respect and sincerity. Generally, when men are talking to women, more eye contact and attentiveness is required.
5. *Etiquette* is a sign of respect. Etiquette does not just mean opening the door for a woman or standing up when she enters the room. To women, etiquette is listening and showing interest.
6. With women, *hard sell does not work.* Salesperson trained for an immediate 'close or lose the order' will not usually succeed. Women, by and large, prefer to explore, compare with one or two other alternatives and thus be totally convinced that they are getting their money's worth. Any attempt to push to finalise a sale makes them more resistant. Around 65 per cent women, as against 45 per cent men, weigh options before making a decision.

Women are less impulsive and place more importance on intuition and judgement about the level of service, features and benefits.

GETTING SALES LEADS

The cost per call is continuously increasing. The greater the number of cold calls and the more the number of salesperson making them, the greater is the wastage. No company can afford this waste of time, effort and money. Thus the attempts to increase sales leads and, consequently, increase the hit rate, thereby increasing the productivity of calls.

What are sales leads? These are names and addresses of customers who have shown an initial interest in your product. How do you get these sales leads? In the US, an enquiry handling service study of 55 million sales leads over five years found that 33 per cent sales leads come from advertising; 22 per cent from public relations; 15 per cent from trade shows and 10 per cent from a toll-free number.

However, most companies find that after receiving these leads, their representatives spend more than 70 per cent of their time setting up appointments, and after all the trouble, find that quite a few of them are useless. What then is the solution to effectively tap the wealth there is in sales leads?

One American company's national sales manager decided to hire a manager and 10 part-time employees (most of them college students) to take over the job of 'sifting' through the leads and setting up appointments for the sales force. The group worked with a database of 1,60,000 leads, used a software programme and now sets up 600 appointments each month. The telemarketers get information about the following:

1. Need of the prospect
2. Time frames
3. Budget
4. Application and use for the product
5. Buying authority
6. The size of their account
7. Whether they currently use the company's product or that of a competitor's

This information is then given to the sales representative making the call. After each appointment, the representative fills out a profile form and sends it back to the marketing department, where it goes into the database for future reference. One month later, a message pops up on the computer screen of the telemarketer, reminding him about a follow-up call and to check if the prospect has any queries or problems. This helps the company to stay in touch with the prospect without wasting the sales representative's time.

A survey in the US shows that of the 300 billion inquiries generated through advertising, public relations, trade shows and events marketing, a mere one-tenth receive a personal follow-up. Approximately 76 per cent of those who inquire about a product intend to buy it; 40 per cent do not even bother to approach the competitor; 63 per cent of all leads turn into a sale within a year.

A structured 'lead system', which should include telemarketing (for which people should be properly trained), enables the sales force to increase its follow-up on leads by four times. Companies also find that their own sales increase with better utilisation of the sales representatives' time. This is more economical in the long run.

A case of a botched follow-up

Coba Pepper Spray is a protective spray developed for use by women. If attacked, they can quickly take the can from their bag and spray into the attacker's eyes. This temporarily blinds him and allows time for the woman to escape from the scene.

As a father of two teenaged girls, I thought this was a good idea. There was a special voucher that was sent with my visa card bill, where cardholders could order up to two cans by phone and would be eligible for a 20 per cent discount. The order would be home delivered.

I phoned and ordered two cans. They promised to deliver within a week. I phoned after two weeks and they could not trace the earlier order. But they took a fresh order and promised to deliver within a week. I waited another fortnight. Nothing happened.

Can you imagine the colossal waste of money in the promotion? The company had lost the sale because of the poor service at the final point of customer contact.

GOOD SALESPEOPLE ARE NOT BORN BUT MADE

Salespeople can build their abilities and strengthen their relations with their customers by doing the following:

1. *Reading*: Find out the latest in your industry. Update yourself by attending courses. Don't always wait to be sponsored by the company. Also update yourself on different topics—astronomy, politics, etc. This not only helps you to be a more knowledgeable person but also more effective in communicating with your prospects who have their own personal likes and interests.
2. *Writing*: Write to the prospect after a meeting to say what you and your company are doing about the prospect's special need or problem. Send him any news cuttings that may be of personal interest to him, or which tell him about your company or his own. This shows you care and could help influence the prospect, especially before an important buying decision.

3. *Team Selling*: If a particular presentation could be enhanced by the presence of an additional person, e.g., a technical person, do coordinate with him for a more effective presentation.
4. *Focussing*: Focus on long-term relationships rather than quick gains. Look at every sale as a long-term relationship. When you do this, you find your attitude towards the prospect changing. You find yourself being more customer-oriented rather than the 'fly by night' type of salesperson.
5. *Involving*: Involve the prospect in identifying his needs and in working out the sales offer—for instance, actually operating a machine while it is being demonstrated.
6. *Taking responsibility*: Take responsibility for errors and misunderstandings even if your company is not really at fault. 'I'm sorry' is a phrase that can be used more often by salespeople. And don't just stop there—go beyond the words and see if you can do something to rectify the error and make up to the customer for the inconvenience he has experienced.
7. *Keeping in touch*: Stay in touch with the customer after a sale. Telephone, write or call on him to find out if all is well, at least once in three to six months. This is of particular importance to sales personnel who sell 'once only' items. Though it is unlikely that the customer will purchase from you again, such being the nature of your product, your service would ensure referrals.
8. *Referrals*: Ask a happy customer for the names of three other individuals who may benefit from your offer, along with the prospect's permission to let you use his name. Doing business with your customer's associates could strengthen the links with your customer.
9. *Letting go*: Let go of a prospect when nothing has happened for a long time, no matter how big the potential is. It may be worth concentrating on new and existing prospects that have a greater potential for success.

THE POWER OF MERCHANDISING

The marketplace today is ever changing, growing more and more competitive all the time, especially in consumer products and consumer durables. Every product is elbowing out every other product, trying to push ahead, get noticed and, finally, get the customer to buy.

It is an old rule in selling that the greater the frequency of the purchase, the smaller the value of the item, the lesser the risk of expensive dissatisfaction and the greater the possibility of the customer being influenced by point of purchase (POP) environments, i.e., the way the product is displayed, the POP material used and display products maintained.

Once the customer has tried a product and is satisfied, there is the possibility that he will remain a customer for a long time. That's how customer franchises are built. Look around you and you will notice the merchandising strength of Johnson & Johnson baby powder, Vicks cough drops and Vaporub ointment, Hamam and Lux toilet soaps, 501 and Rin washing soaps, Wills cigarettes, Comfit and Stayfree sanitary napkins, and so many others. This powerful merchandising does not occur by accident. It is implemented by design.

These salesperson know the power of merchandising. They ensure that their product is displayed in the right quantities and at the right position in the shop—at eye level and just behind the counter. They understand that the product itself is the most important POP material. That it should be kept dust free and presentable even if it means cleaning up some of the stock with a duster themselves.

They know that they have to put up display material themselves and do so sensibly, and not just hand it over to the dealer with a request to put it up later. When this is done, the high-quality paper posters end up being used as book covers by the dealers' children rather than as POP material to help sell the product.

These salesperson know that it is better to have a good display in fewer outlets, rather than spread the butter thin and have just one piece in every outlet where it may not even be noticed. They know that the POP material has to be maintained—torn posters removed, broken danglers cut out. You cannot allow poor POP material to project a poor image of your product.

These salesperson know that merchandising is an integral part of the selling job. It is not an 'extra'. It is not a burden. It is not an appendage. It is what makes selling more effective and, in the long run, makes selling easier.

Three aspects that make merchandising a success are as follows:

1. *The design of the package* itself, so that it stands out on the shelf. Great care has to be taken in terms of graphics and colours. These have to also identify with the product category. It is such a pleasure to pass by a store, even while sitting in a bus, and still notice products such as Surf detergent, Wills cigarettes, Peter Scot Whisky, Ariel and many others. But a far greater number of products are unnoticeable even when one has entered the store and the product is lying on shelves at eye level.
2. The *awareness among salesperson* that merchandising is a part of their job and helps sell more than would otherwise be possible. Salesperson tend to think of their assignment in very restricted terms of 'order booking'. Merchandising and development of new customers are considered to be an additional burden imposed by the company, for which they cannot find the time and, more important, the inclination.

   The stockist will not undertake the job when he finds that the salesperson himself is taking it so lightly. Millions of rupees spent on promotion material are lost and the top management in companies is blissfully ignorant of this large preventable waste in the marketplace.
3. The *appreciation among retailers* that merchandising is a necessary ingredient in retailing, that effective merchandising helps them to present a better public appearance and sell more. At present most retailers are not 'house proud'. They feel that all merchandising is a favour to the manufacturer with nothing in it for them and that, therefore, all merchandising activity should be paid for and supported by the manufacturer.

As salesperson themselves have not been properly trained or their attitudes have not been changed by their companies, they, in turn, are not able to transmit a positive attitude towards merchandising to the retailers. In this aspect, the salesperson becomes the first stumbling block in the progress of the company. Because he is not convinced himself, he cannot convince the retailer. The result is a general reluctance all around. The retailer then begins to find a display contest unattractive, resents posters and other materials cluttering his shop, feels disappointed when he does not win a prize from a contest and, therefore, does not want the salesperson to mess around with stocks in his shelf.

Where the product is the main POP

Arun was a salesperson for a large biscuit company. He and I were waiting for the bus to take us home from Flora Fountain in Mumbai. We had just finished the day's work, covering 40 outlets in the business district. All through the day, I had been observing Arun's strengths and weaknesses. He was warm and friendly with dealers, he had a proper route plan, he knew what he was going to achieve and where. After all, he had been working in the same area and in the same company for nearly 12 years.

But there was one flaw. Arun had excellent merchandising material in his bag, including danglers, posters and stickers. He selectively gave some of these to the better retail outlets with the request that they put them up later, whenever and wherever convenient. Perhaps they did or perhaps they didn't. It was more likely the latter. If Arun would not take the trouble to stop and put up his own company's display material, why should they?

As we stood there at the bus stop that evening, there was this young man carefully putting up books for sale on his pavement stall, taking care to see that the titles were visible, the colours contrasted, and that they were easy for a customer to pick up and browse through. Close by, a fruit vendor had a small stall with neatly piled up bananas, apples and guavas. And he was busy polishing the apples in the top row to give them an inviting shine.

And as we looked on, Arun and I were getting the message of how effective good merchandising is and a demonstration of people doing it well because they have understood its power through sheer experience.

EXTRA SERVICES

Industrial products

A company in Chennai bought a double cone mixer from Seal in Delhi because they quoted the lowest rate compared to parties in Mumbai. The specifications were agreed to and the mixer arrived. Six months later, the cap and the rim showed signs of rusting. A complaint was lodged with the supplier. He wrote back a nice letter saying they would be happy to send a replacement if the company could first send the defective part back to Delhi. In the meantime, the mixer would have to lie idle, perhaps for one or two months, till the replacement was received, and that was the company's problem not Seal's. And Seal did not have any representative in Chennai.

Some time later, the company bought a capsule disintegrator machine from Taps in Mumbai. A few months later, the disintegrator stopped working. Afraid to get anyone else to touch the machine during the guarantee period, the company wrote to Taps asking them to send an engineer to repair the machine. 'Sorry, we do not have such arrangements' was the response. 'If you can send the machine to Mumbai, we will certainly attend to the repairs.'

These companies, like many others, forgot that selling does not stop with the sale and the collection of money. With industrial products and consumer durables, real selling starts after the sale is made. After-sales service also plays a vital role in the selling of services, as with insurance agents or advertising agencies.

Consumer durables

All reputed air conditioner manufacturers will offer free after-sales service for a certain period of time and paid service after that. The customer then has a choice in this matter and cannot complain. If one chooses to buy from an individual who puts parts together to create an air conditioner, one will certainly get it cheaper, but there could be trouble. There may be no service and one may not even be able to locate the supplier in case of any major problem later.

Major typewriter manufacturers offer after-sales service in nearly all major towns and so do reputed machinery suppliers, and vehicle and tool manufacturers. The reason for the success of some kitchen mixers has not only been their design and motor, but also their extensive service organisation.

Insurance

Most insurance agents disappear after they have signed up a client for a life insurance policy. Very few think of maintaining a file for each client, reminding them of the dates of payment, checking at intervals if any further policy is to be bought, arranging for loans against the policy and other such after-sales services. Those who do, build up a large clientele over a period of time. Those who don't, keep looking out for the occasional unsuspecting customer who will be their next victim, then sell to him quickly and again slink back into anonymity.

Computers

Computer companies have always been ahead of everyone else in this respect. Initially, computers were so expensive that few could afford to buy one. So they sold computer time. In order to do this successfully, the computer salesperson had to find out all about the potential customer's business, see how they could use computer time and benefit from it, and guide the customer's employees to make optimum use of the computer—a very real after-sales service.

Elevators

Perhaps the best and quickest after-sales service systems are to be found in the elevator business. Elevators have to be necessarily kept 'in trim'. If something does go wrong, it has to be set right immediately. It cannot wait too long. Therefore, more than in any other product area, the decision on the elevator brand will be guided more by the brand status and the after-sales service record than by the price or other considerations.

Lessons to be learned

After-sales service is what distinguishes one brand from another. The brand name tells the customer about not only the quality and benefits of the product but also the kind of after-sales service which he will receive. It is an indication that the manufacturer genuinely believes that the sale is the beginning of a relationship, not the end of one. Perhaps we have something to learn from brands like Citizen and Sanyo. Their products were not available in India, or manufactured and imported in any organised fashion. Many individuals bought them abroad and brought them into the country. The Japanese manufacturers felt an obligation to ensure that proper after-sales service is provided even in India. Hence the identification of establishments (in the print media advertisements marked 'for information only') authorised to provide this service on the company's behalf.

CUSTOMER SATISFACTION MUST FOR SURVIVAL

'We live in critical times in which there are only two types of companies—quality companies and companies which will be beaten, eliminated or taken over by quality companies,' says Dr Rene T. Domingo in a recent article in the *World Executive's Digest*. Quality, he says, is no longer an option. It is a must for survival.

Among the four areas he mentions where quality is critical, the first one is what concerns the salesperson of today, and that is the customer's supremacy. According to him, the first target the company has to aim at continuously is its customers and their changing needs and wants. Increasing purchasing power enables them to choose from among the sellers, and with their tastes becoming more and more sophisticated, customers are in a constant state of dissatisfaction.

Are customers loyal? Customers today want value for their money. If this happens, they are likely to be loyal. However, we can no longer sit back and count on their loyalty. We have to keep striving for more and more ways to keep them happy and satisfied. If we do not keep improving, we are in danger of losing them to the competition.

Toyota is an example of customer satisfaction being practised by a company and its employees. A manager of an Asian subsidiary of Toyota believed that the work of his department was to retain customers indefinitely, so that

- the second and third cars of the customer would be Toyotas;
- cars of other members of his family would also be Toyotas;
- the customer would renew his car, every three to four years, with another Toyota.

However, what does an employee do when his company is not really geared to customer satisfaction, but he personally believes in it? Many of us know that for most government organisations in India, customer service is nothing more than a placard on a wall.

It was therefore a pleasant surprise for me to have a problem solved over the telephone in five minutes, thanks to the courtesy and helpfulness of a divisional manager of the National Insurance Company, all because he was personally committed to customer satisfaction.

The ideal case, therefore, would be for both the company and the employee to believe in customer satisfaction. However, if the company does not really practise it, the professional salesperson of today must do his utmost to put it into practice—for his own survival and the company's.

Ron Willingham in the book *Hey, I'm the Customer* recommends that we think on the lines of 'You are the customer, you pay my salary.' This will help us perceive customers in an objective light and make us go all out to satisfy and retain them.

TOTAL CUSTOMER SATISFACTION: MYTH OR REALITY

There is another marketing fallacy which all salespersons should be wary of—'*You must provide 100 per cent customer satisfaction*.' This is a myth.

In our anxiety to provide customer satisfaction, many of us are in danger of going overboard. Why? Because, with all due respect to valued customers, the more service you give them, the more they want. It is the concept behind the Japanese theme of 'Going beyond customer satisfaction, to creating customer delight.'

There is nothing wrong with the basic theme. In fact, everything is right about it. But you have to be careful. The satisfaction must tie up with the price and delight must be tied up with a higher price. Both must be clearly spelt out to the customer in advance, so that he knows what he is getting or not getting.

Customer demands will never cease. They have a right to ask. The company in turn has many duties to perform, first and foremost to the customer, then to the shareholders, employees, government and the community. The company cannot satisfy the demands of one stakeholder at the cost of another. All four or five have to be balanced. It should be profitable to all of them, although primarily to the customer, who must perceive the product as good value for money.

When the level of customer satisfaction reaches around 90 to 92 per cent, the cost of providing additional satisfaction increases disproportionately to the value that it will provide to the company. The law of diminishing returns begins to operate and at that point in the graph, you need to put a stop.

There will be customers who will be unhappy. There will be those who demand much more than you have promised. There will be those who try to make fraudulent claims. There will be those who make every sales call of the salesperson an experience in purgatory.

The salesperson cannot be all things to all people. If he is everything to 90 per cent of his customers, all is right with him and the world. If he tries to overstep and give away what the company cannot afford to give, except at a loss, in terms of either product value addition, lower price or faster distribution, then the salesperson would be looking after the interests of only the customer while being paid a salary by the company. The salesperson needs to be fair to both his customer and his company, and constantly remember that complete customer satisfaction is a myth.

CUSTOMER SERVICE FOR SUCCESS TODAY AND TOMORROW

There was an article recently on how a Singapore-based designer clothes company, Giordano, increased the company turnover by 64 per cent in one year. According to the founder of Giordano Jimmy Lai says, as a retailer, the product is half of what they sell, the other half being service. Their volumes are so high that they have to get customers to come back, and good service is the best way to get them to return.

For businesses with retail outlets, it would help to remember that Giordano considers frontline workers as its customer service heroes. It believes that even the most sophisticated training programme won't guarantee the best customer service. People are the key. They make exceptional customer service possible. Training is merely a skeleton of a customer service programme. It's the people who deliver it that give it form and meaning.

It is interesting to note some of the qualities of a few of their exceptional frontline workers.

1. The values taught and instilled by the family are reflected in their lives and work—*values of caring, sharing and giving.* Having a difficult childhood, pitching in to supplement the

family income, with the mother working hard to support four children, helped one of the star performers learn the gift of *patience*. Patience is a great virtue for a salesperson of today in dealing with difficult and rude customers.

2. Seeing a parent work hard and/or having to work as a child to supplement the family income, helped some of them to develop a *respect for work*.
3. They are *good natured and charming* in one way or another and have the ability to be in control of their moods, i.e., to be *proactive* instead of reactive.

   Being proactive means being responsible for our own lives. It means to have the initiative and responsibility to make things happen. Proactive people don't blame circumstances, others, conditions, weather, etc., for their behaviour. Their behaviour is a result of a choice based on values rather than feelings.

   The opposite of proactive is reactive, i.e., you react to a situation or person without deliberation or thought. It is tough being proactive because of years of being reactive, but we can start today. Take one day at a time, and see how many times you were proactive or reactive. Let's learn to be better people and thereby better salespeople.
4. *They see their job from the customer's point of view*. No effort will be spared to try and satisfy even the most difficult customer. As one of the salespersons says, 'When I'm with a customer, irrespective of whether he's buying something or not, I ask myself, if I were the customer, how would I like to be served and treated?'
5. They have *no hesitation in doing even menial jobs*, whenever a need arises. There are therefore no prejudices and hang-ups of 'this is not a part of my job' variety.
6. They *tend to have a hobby*, such as painting and music, which provides an outlet for emotions and creativity.
7. They often *join clubs* and *committees*, which help them develop leadership skills and team building. These are the skills that get tested on the shop floor.
8. They learn to *see the humorous and funny side of things*. A sense of humour is something one can cultivate and learn. Some people just have it in them, but learning to see the funny side can diffuse the most tense and stressful of situations.

Companies and salespeople interested in customer service could perhaps learn from Giordano's company policy for customer service, which involves the following:

- *Greeting*: Making the customer feel welcome the minute he walks into the store.
- *Merchandise presentation.*
- *Selling up*: Giving the customer additional product information on new arrivals, promotional items, etc.
- *Closing*: Focussing on speed and accuracy.

The 'Giordano Means Service' philosophy has three laws:

1. We welcome unlimited trials, i.e., there is no bar on the number of shirts a customer can try, until he is satisfied with the product.
2. We exchange, no questions asked.
3. We serve with a smile.

Obviously, Giordano's is truly a success story and a visit to their store an experience in itself.

BUILDING TRUST

A Japanese example

A gentleman visiting Japan bought a tape recorder, but when he went back to his hotel and tried it out, he found it was not working. He rang up the store, told them his problem and said that he had just three hours before leaving for the airport.

The store manager said they would look after this and within an hour sent a service man with a replacement. When the original equipment was checked, it was found that there was nothing wrong with it, but the service man insisted that the gentleman take the new one and showed him how to operate it. As he said, 'We don't want you leave Japan with the feeling that Japanese products are inferior and that they don't work.' This is the essence of after-sales service and an example of pride in one's product and in one's country.

A Swiss example

There is scope for implementation of after-sales service even in consumables as shown by the legend on a box of Lindt & Sprüngli chocolates from Switzerland. It gives the Lindt Quality Guarantee signed by Rudolf Sprüngli and asks the customer to write back in case there is any complaint, with details of where the box was bought. It adds that the company would be happy to have the box replaced because Lindt has been making chocolates since 1845 and insists on providing the customer with the best. Such a guarantee of after-sales service builds confidence and then builds sales.

A lack of trust

Every evening, Ramesh is at the traffic lights where Churchgate Street joins Marine Drive. The stream of cars does not stop till late into the night, all heading for their homes in north Mumbai. Ramesh operates at this junction, selling roses to car owners on their way home. They have the ability to pay. It is also a captive audience. They are there, waiting for the lights to change to green.

Ramesh gives priority to cars with couples as he knows that he can pressurise the man to buy a dozen roses for his wife or, better still, his date. He offers them the roses at Rs 12 for a dozen. No response. He reduces the price to Rs 10. Only a slight hint of interest. The lights will turn green at any moment. 'All right, Rs 8,' he says. The lights have changed. 'Rs 6 is my last price—they are fresh roses and will last for two days!'

But it's too late. The car has moved on and the prospect's confidence has been shattered. 'The price has changed too much, too soon. Never trust these flower sellers. Perhaps, they are stolen flowers anyway!'

There is a lesson to be learnt in selling, whether flowers or heavy machinery. Selling is building trust and relationships.

SALESMANSHIP—A CAREER, NOT A STEPPING STONE

In the 1950s, Lance Noronha was a star salesperson for May and Baker in Mumbai. A likeable person with an engaging smile, he had as big a following among theatre lovers (he was active on the English amateur stage) as among his customers. What many colleagues never forgot about him was that he was offered a promotion to the position of a sales manager twice, but he turned it down both times. He said he enjoyed selling and was not cut out to guide and lead other salesperson. He wanted to be footloose and fancy-free. It was the judgement of a man who knew how much his reach matched his grasp.

Why do many salesperson who have crossed 45 constantly keep grumbling with the refrain 'how many years am I going to carry this bag?' Why does every salesperson feel that he must graduate to carrying an executive briefcase, and that if he has not made it, then his life has been a total failure? Why do salesperson always look upon the assignment as a stepping stone to being a sales executive, rather than as a career, just like any other?

There are many reasons for this situation prevailing in India. The problem has been with the attitude of salesperson themselves as well as the management. Both have made an effective contribution towards polluting the environment and giving a wrong direction to sales skills as a career.

Salesperson in India are brought up in an environment where selling is considered infra dig. Therefore, hardly anyone in school or college really thinks of going into selling as a career. They meander into it more by accident than by design. When they are in the field, people refer to them as 'agents' and talk about the selling profession in derogatory tones. The salesperson then wants to escape from this label. Consequently, he will never suggest that his son become a salesperson, even if he has the aptitude to be one. This is a sad reflection of a lack of pride in the profession.

Not every lawyer becomes a legal counsel and not every doctor a medical consultant. This is an accepted fact of life. Those who have not progressed continue to do their best and excel as lawyers or doctors. But a salesperson who does not become a sales manager feels that he has reached 'the end of the road' and that his life has been one big failure. Very seldom does the salesperson continue in his profession with an attitude of wanting to excel in what he is doing.

All this is so, probably because salesperson have never really looked upon selling as a career and a profession. This is why there is no professional body of salesperson. There are unions which fight for better wages, less work, workers' rights and such other benefits. But these unions take no action to encourage professionalism in selling. This situation is bound to change in the 21st century.

MAINTAINING FAMILY TIES

Travel is an important part of a salesperson's life. Very few have territories within city limits. For most, outstation travel involves at least 50 per cent of their working month. Although at the start one enjoys the chance to see new places and meet new people, many find that after a while it tends to get monotonous and physically tiring. To keep in touch with home becomes difficult. For the married salesperson, juggling his job/travel and his family life is often very difficult. Spouses and children suffer from loneliness, fear of possible illnesses, and accidents or even death of the salesperson while he is away.

Reunions sometimes cause more anxiety because each side is looking forward to fulfilling his/her need. The husband may be looking forward to putting up his feet and relaxing after a 10-day strenuous tour, while the wife and children might be looking forward to him taking them out, since they've been cooped up in the house while he's been away. The situation becomes more complicated when the tired traveller needs to attend to bills or a broken household appliance.

How can couples and their children best deal with this separation caused by business travel?

1. Try to maintain the salesperson's participation in the family by telephone or letter.
2. Recognise and talk about conflicts that arise because of the traveller's absence.
3. To reduce conflict, try and avoid business travel on important family occasions.
4. Use predetermined times to call home.
5. Those at home should use the salesperson's absence as an opportunity to indulge in personal preferences in meals, entertainment and activities.

With wives also working now, this problem will increase, but with proper care and planning, travellers and their families can help lessen the pain and inconvenience of business travel.

The sales manager of a direct selling company was asked to give the secret of hiring successful salesperson. He said, 'I check on the applicant's appearance very closely. If I find that his trousers show more wear than his shoes, I don't hire him because he is making too many contacts in the wrong places!'

HUMILITY AND HONESTY

Author Mark H. McCormack in his famous book *What They Don't Teach You at Harvard Business School* makes certain comments about people who say certain things because they wrongly assume that they are creating the right impression. In his experience the three most difficult phrases for people to say are as follows:

1. *I don't know*: Do people not want to say this because they might appear ignorant to others? It does require honesty and courage to say this but this self-effacing approach is almost always more effective than the know-it-all approach.
2. *I need help*: This is another phrase which people are afraid to voice as it will make them look inadequate in their job. Since business organisations are structured for work to be done in teams, it will be difficult for a 'Lone Ranger' to function well without saying 'I need help'.
3. *I was wrong*: The higher one goes in life, the more difficult it is to admit one's mistake. The chairman of a medium-sized company complained about his frustrations over the conservative attitude of his management-level employees. 'The problem, he said, is that they're all afraid to make a mistake.'

To move forward, one needs to take risks and this encompasses a certain amount of failure. The people who are least secure about their abilities have the hardest time admitting their mistakes. They fail to realise that making a mistake and admitting it are two totally separate acts. It is not the mistake itself, but how a mistake is handled that forms the lasting impression.

To be better a person, these three hard-to-say phrases need to be incorporated in one's way of thinking, particularly for the salesperson to become better at his job.

NEED TO BUILD SELF-ESTEEM

Self-esteem is the value we place in ourselves. It involves living our lives according to that value.

Having a high self-esteem is viewing ourselves as we do our loved ones—as precious and deserving the best. How many of us think of ourselves that way? Having a high self-esteem also means putting our own needs first sometimes. In the beginning you feel a little uncomfortable with putting yourself first; you feel selfish. But by giving to ourselves we recharge the batteries that enable us to continue giving to others.

Self-esteem does not remain constant all the time. When we've done something good and everything goes well, our self-esteem rises. But when things go badly and we have failed, it drops.

Do a simple exercise for yourself. List all your positive points, on one side, and the negative, on the other. At the end of the exercise, check which side has more points. If the side listing your positive points is longer, you have healthy self-esteem. If, however, your list of negative points is longer, the following six tools , if used regularly, can help build and sustain positive self-esteem.

1. *Keep commitments*: Commitments are of two kinds—to others and to ourselves. The ones made to others are easier to keep because they are 'public'. But the ones made to ourselves, e.g., making of a minimum of eight calls per day or leaving the house at 9.00 am sharp every morning, are the ones we may not keep. Sometimes we don't entirely give our best, for instance, we show up five minutes late or post our daily report just a day later. These are things in which we cheat ourselves of feeling great about ourselves.

   Since most of us have trouble keeping commitments, the trick is to make only those commitments that we know we'll keep. Thus we begin keeping a track record of successes rather than failures. Set deadlines for yourself and avoid postponements.
2. *Take Risks*: Taking risks makes us feel good when we succeed, and if we fail, we have at least grown wiser by facing uncertainties. Taking a big risk all at once is not a good idea but breaking the risk into manageable sections and 'small steps' helps.

   Being specific also helps. For instance, instead of saying 'I want to risk being less shy', set up a specific plan for a week—'I will speak to two strangers before Wednesday.' Risks can be big or small, but consciously bringing them into our lives is a way of feeling better.
3. *Make Changes*: Change is one of the most important features of life. If we constantly keep changing small things in our life, we will have better control of our lives and, therefore, also be more open to change in our profession as well as the world around us, which is changing much faster than most of us want. For instance, change in our waking habits by waking up

15 minutes earlier and exercising, praying, jogging or just deep breathing.

4. *Forgive ourselves*: Expecting perfection from ourselves all the time may not be realistic. We are human and often fail. We can't build self-esteem by punishing or being angry with ourselves, no matter how big a mistake we've made. The faster we forgive ourselves, see how and where we have failed, and take some action not to repeat the mistake, the faster we move on.
5. *Forgive Others*: Anger, resentment, jealousy and other uncomfortable feelings not only separate us from others but also keep us in a stew. Learning to let go of such feelings is critical to high self-esteem. This does not mean that you cannot have negative feelings or that you should deny them, but what it does mean is that you should not continue to 'hang on to them'. They can only help destroy and not build your self-esteem.

   How then can we cope with unpleasant feelings which need to be expressed? Not expressing them can build up a lot of stress and resentment. Perhaps one way is to write a letter to the person concerned, for the written word can express your feelings better than verbal conversation. Another way, especially when tension is high and the feelings are very strong, is to write a letter expressing all that we feel but not send it. The unsent letter works especially well for those whom we are not ready to confront.
6. *Take credit*: Focussing on our good points is one of the most effective ways of enhancing self-esteem. This does not mean being boastful. Boasting is usually a sign that someone doesn't feel good about himself. Making a list of 10 qualities we like about ourselves and sharing this list with our family or spouse can prove to be fun and insightful. When we are ready to accept the good points about ourselves, we will also begin to readily acknowledge others for their gifts.

   Self-esteem is not a destination but a process or skill. As with any other skill, we are better at it on some days, but without practice, we grow rusty. With practice, anyone can become good at maintaining a high, healthy self-esteem.

AN ABILITY TO GIVE

All salesperson know that they can never have a perfect product —a product that is the best in the market in terms of quality, with the lowest price, the widest distribution and the highest level of promotion. If there were such a product, there would be no need for salesperson. The product would sell by itself. Because it is the very best, there is no competition, at least not on the same level.

Therefore, each product or service concentrates on its strengths, at the same time trying to reduce its weaknesses. Each gets the customer to buy on the basis of strengths that make it the preferred product, based on the needs and wants of that particular customer.

It is the same with salesperson. No salesperson is perfect. No salesperson has all the strengths and none of the weaknesses. He must surely try to overcome some or all of his weaknesses. But it is unlikely he will ever be good at everything. He will, therefore, have to identify his strengths and capitalise on them. In some ways, the salesperson will then occupy a niche in the customer's mind, just like a product.

Some salesperson are excellent at product knowledge. Over 30 years ago in Jabalpur, there was a medical representative Rodricks who was invited to address the local IMA (Indian Medical Association) once every year on 'Recent Advances in Antibiotic Therapy'. That was his speciality. He was so good at it that he knew more on this particular subject than most doctors did, even though he was not a doctor.

There was a salesperson named Ahluwalia in Indore whose product knowledge was below par. However, his calm manner and a spontaneous sense of humour made him so lovable and welcome to customers that they bought his product even though he could not answer all their questions. They had to refer to the product literature later.

There was a salesperson named Dhareshwar in Belgaum, Karnataka, who was an excellent numerologist. Many doctors in the whole area waited for him to make his call so that they could also consult him about their personal matters.

Salesperson Prakash in Ahmedabad sent birthday cards to all his customers. He never forgot their birthdays. And the customers, in turn, never forgot him or his products.

There are different ways to salvation. And there are different ways for success in selling. Each one of us has to trade on his innate strengths and capitalise on them, while at the same time working to correct the weaknesses.

RESISTING PEER PRESSURE

All of us are subjected to peer pressure in school, college, the neighbourhood and our work life.

A child may want a perfumed eraser because his friend has one. A college student may want baggy trousers because the other boys wear those and he feels left out. He will perhaps not be happy until he also buys and wears one. The wife may be under peer pressure to buy an expensive sari for a certain function because some women in the family or the neighbourhood may be buying a *kanjeevaram* for the occasion.

It happens to all of us, and it happens to salesperson. Most salesperson work alone. They are either at the headquarters, which may not be their hometowns, or away from headquarters on tour for long periods of time. They live in hotels, dormitories or guesthouses. And most salesperson congregate at the same places to stay in, to meet and have a chat. And that is where peer pressure begins to be exerted. It is here that the salesperson is tempted to abide by the unwritten laws laid down by the peer group and gets to

- making only a limited number of customer calls, although he could easily make more, most days of the week;
- closing early and starting late, as a result of a spending the night playing cards or imbibing alcohol;
- dropping off the most important customers who are the most difficult to meet;
- limiting the sales achievement, so that targets for next year will be based on a lower sales figure for this year.

It is always difficult to fight peer pressure and easier to succumb to it—to fall in line and then to be among the average performers. It is at the beginning of the salesperson's career that the foundation is laid for him to either accept peer pressure and belong to the majority or resist it to be his own man, keep his own counsel, be different and move on to greater achievement and glory.

Industriousness, planning and knowledge are the keys to success. Instead of saying 'I certainly handled that situation cleverly', say

'How could I have handled that situation more effectively?' Instead of thinking 'I did a great day's work today', say 'What did I do today that could have been done better?'

A study of 624 salespersons in the US showed that 90 per cent of salespersons who fail insist that they work hard. This is human. We think we are utilising our full potential to get every paisa of business from the territory being covered. The results of the survey are interesting and of significance to any salesperson aspiring for leadership. The survey found the following weaknesses among the salesperson:

Weaknesses	No. of Salespersons	Percentage
Lack of industry	196	31
Failure to follow instructions	72	12
Inadequate knowledge	72	12
Lack of fighting spirit	64	10
Lack of determination	64	10
Dishonesty	52	8
Lack of enthusiasm	28	4
Lack of tact and courtesy	28	4
Drinking or gambling	24	3
Poor health	4	1
Others	20	5

HANDLING STRESS

If you are regularly stressed out at work, psychologists begin to suspect that it is not the work but the worker who may be responsible for a large part of the stress. It has been observed that people with stress-prone personalities get worked up even in relatively low-pressure jobs.

The following categories of people are more stress prone at work:

1. *People who want predictability at all times.*
   Continuity-loving workers, who feel out of control and upset when something requires them to change their thinking or routine, even if there is no threat. Psychologists suggest that such people expect something unforeseen every working day and expect some changes in the planned order of work.
2. *People who are perfectionists.* Perfectionists have to realise, especially with respect to time management, that it is better to get a job done, with small imperfections, than not to get it

done at all! They must also remember that some factors are uncontrollable.

3. *People who cannot say 'no' to others and push their own personal needs to the back.* Working mothers are more prone to suffer stress with regard to this. Experts suggest that you put your own needs in a fair priority rating along with all the jobs to be done. When it is time to meet those needs, do them full justice and without guilt!

   Psychologists now believe that it is not so much what happens that causes emotions—it is what we tell ourselves about them.

SELF-ANALYSIS THROUGH SALES REPORTS

Sales reports, tour plans, customer coverage plans, customer profiles, customer classifications, daily plans of work, daily reports, competitor activity reports, monthly review reports—all these help the salesperson to analyse, keep learning and continuously improve.

Sales reports will help the salesperson more than they help the company. Reports mirror the salesperson's work to himself as well as project the quality and quantity of his work to a faraway office.

Here is a quick-response questionnaire on sales reports, which will help you to understand and appreciate how the reports you are required to fill help you to do a better and more effective job.

1.	A salesperson is paid to do a selling job and produce sales, not write sales reports.	True/False
2.	The reports we have are too descriptive and should be changed to an objective system.	True/False
3.	The salesperson is too tired at the end of the day to sit and write reports.	True/False
4.	The reports are seldom read by the office and, therefore, are just a waste of the salesperson's time.	True/False
5.	Even when the reports are read, the territory knowledge of the office staff is so little that the reports become meaningless to them.	True/False

(Continued)

(Continued)

6.	Insistence on reports only shows that the office does not trust the salesperson.	True/False
7.	A good alternative would be for the salespersons to maintain a diary. Office executives can check this on every visit. Then the daily/weekly report is not necessary.	True/False
8.	Office executives complain that they find our handwritten reports difficult to read.	True/False
9.	When we commit sales figures or orders in our reports, with good intentions, the office pins us down and quotes from our reports.	True/False
10.	In our kind of selling, business matures after a long time and with continuous visits. Sending reports with just a mention of visits is, therefore, a poor indicator of what exactly is happening.	True/False

The following sales report forms have been provided at the end of this chapter (these may be amended based on your needs):

1. Monthly Tour Plan
2. Daily Plan of Work
3. Monthly Customer Call Analysis
4. Field Work Analysis
5. Monthly Review

Report 1

Month	Year

Monthly Tour Plan

Name & Designation	
Depot	
Territory	
Regional Office	

Date	Markets						Target Qty. MT	Achieved Qty. MT	Price	Reali-sation	Remarks
	1	2	3	4	5	6					
1											
2											
3											
4											
5											
6											
27											
28											
29											
30											
31											

*To be filled on 25th of previous month by

Duplicate for approval

Signature	
Date of Submission	
Name of Supervisor	
Designation	

Report 2

Month	Year

Name & Designation	
Depot	
Territory	
Regional Office	

Daily Plan of Work

Time	Place	Customer	Objective	Result/Remarks	Next Visit
0900 hrs					
1000					
1100					
1600					
1700					

(Copies of DPW will be the Weekly Report to Area/Regional Office)

To bo fillod by

Signature	
Date of Submission	
Name of Supervisor	
Designation	

Report 3

Month	Year

Monthly Customer Call Analysis Report

Name & Designation	
Depot	
Territory	
Regional Office	

Month	Trade	Productive	Institution	Productive	Others	Productive	Total	Productive	Remarks
Apr									
May									
Feb									
Mar									
Total									

Productive = When orders are booked during the visit.

To be filled by and submitted by 5th of next month.

Signature	
Date of Submission	
Name of Supervisor	
Designation	

Report 4

Month	Year

Name & Designation	
Depot	
Territory	
Regional Office	

Field Work Analysis

Month	1	2	3	4	5	6	7	8	9	10	11	12	13	14	15	16	17	18	19	20	21	22	23	24	25	26	27	28	29	30	31
Apr																															
May																															
Jun																															
Jan																															
Feb																															
Mar																															
Total																															

Legend

Put initials of person worked with/or write 'self' if worked alone.

To be filled by and submitted to immediate supervisor by 5th of next month.

Signature	
Date of Submission	
Name of Supervisor	
Designation	

Report 5

Month	Year

Monthly Review Meeting Performance

Name & Designation	
Depot	
Territory	
Regional Office	

Name		Territory Coverage	Sales	Realisation	Outstanding No. of Days	Call Avg.	Tech. Q	Selling Q.	Total Marks	Remarks (Actions for improvement)
	Marks	10	20	20	20	10	10	10	100	
1										
2										
3										
4										
17										
18										
19										
20										

Reporting

Signature	
Date of Submission	
Name of Supervisor	
Designation	

CHAPTER 11

Selling in the 21st Century

COORDINATED TEAM EFFORTS

Gone are the days when a salesperson could work alone, when it was one salesperson and one customer in a single relationship. Sometimes relationships were so strong that when the salesperson left the company to join a competitor, he could very easily carry the customer with him to his new employer. Such things still happen but not as frequently.

In much of today's selling, you need teamwork. People in different functions must work together and produce a synergistic effect. This is particularly so in the selling of industrial products, services or projects where teamwork is the key to success.

This is why in industrial or services selling you can have so many situations, such as:

1. One salesperson catering to one customer.
2. One salesperson catering to a group of customer personnel.
3. A group of sales personnel catering to one customer.
4. A group of sales personnel catering to a group of customer personnel.
5. A panel of sales personnel (seminar selling) catering to a large number of customers/personnel.

Industrial products salespersons are often accompanied by personnel from their R&D, production, technical support services or after-sales service departments. Even consumer product salespersons have to now work in coordination with the product management team from the head office so that there is a correlation between advertising campaigns and extra loading of stocks, between distribution of merchandising material and display of stock on shelves, and between the many other coordination activities that are required.

'No man is an island unto himself' is a general rule for all human beings, but even more relevant to those of us in the profession of selling.

THE KEY—KNOWING THE CUSTOMER'S CUSTOMER

It takes a lot of time and effort to know the customer's customer. To study his needs and wants. And then to offer your customer a product or service that will help him tailor his product/service to the needs of his customers. The fit is then perfect. Your customer will be able to build a bond with his customer. And you will be able to build a bond with your customer.

It is on such foundations that long-term relations are built. These are not 'friendship clubs'. These are naturally beneficial associations. And this is what honest selling is all about.

However, this means spending time to study the market segments of your customer's customers as if they were your own customers. Then, you would have to work backwards to see how you can tailor your offering to fit into his offering to his customers. It can be a grade of steel or it could be a box of chocolates. It is a 'downstream study' for upstream and successful marketing.

The salespersons who do this will be the flag bearers for salesmanship in the 21st century.

TECHNOLOGY FOR GREATER EFFECTIVENESS

In the 1960s and 1970s, salespersons wrote their reports by hand. They used carbon paper to make four or five copies. The last one, kept as a file copy for oneself, was invariably illegible because it was so faint. Salespersons in the more sophisticated and progressive companies like Glaxo were provided with portable typewriters. The British bosses ensured that they could read the reports without being at the mercy of poor handwriting.

In the 1990s, salespersons had many advantages. They could use pagers so that they could be contacted wherever they were in the market. They were not required to report to the office at a fixed time everyday. Today, salespersons who sell 'high ticket' items can use cell phones. They can make and receive calls conveniently wherever they are. Salespersons can also use dictaphones, now available in small sizes, to dictate summaries of conversations, points for actions or special requests, which can then be converted into written reports. Using a laptop will become de rigueur for salespersons. They can then have their journey plan, customer profile, classification, call frequency chart, daily plan, daily report, competitive market activity report, monthly analysis and customer sales record all logged in and easily available, updated and transmitted to the office.

The salesperson is able to do more in the time available or do better by using technology to reduce the load of routine.

MARKETING IN THE 21st CENTURY

This is what Philip Kotler has to say about marketing in the new millennium, in an interview to *The Economic Times*, India.

> Marketing media in the new millennia will have more capability to move the shopper from awareness, interest, preference to purchase—unlike advertising which didn't make the last step.
>
> The marketplace in the new millennium: More customers are likely to work and shop from home. Teleshopping will become a daily routine. To the extent that more work can be done from home, work opportunities are likely to migrate to lower cost countries. Consumers will have much more information available with electronic catalogues, Internet malls et al. This will let them pay more rationally and price sensitively. The new millennium will see a situation of almost unlimited choice.
>
> Production: I see more modular production structures which will simultaneously enable the customer to get more variety and the manufacturer to operate at lower costs. It will also allow mass-customisation. More products are likely to use microprocessors—like the E-type Mercedes. It incorporates 31 microprocessors; the windshield wipers, for instance, work automatically when rain starts.
>
> New marketing capacities: I see the proliferation of customer databases. These are more reliable than market surveys since they actually capture buying behaviour. Data warehouses and data mining will become the norm. Media will become more targeted. Thousands of magazines, direct mail and the Internet will permit more customised and personalised information. Activity based costing is likely to pick up, making it easier to identify high volume, high profit customers and develop customer loyalty individually.

> Distribution: I see dematerialisation as the norm. More at home purchasing, coupled with consumers downloading music, film, software and books. All these are information products, and as a consequence, 'shops' will be open 24 hours a day, seven days a week.
>
> Some more general trends in marketing: A significant reduction in field sales forces and more reliance on media-based communications. Trade shows are likely to be replaced by electronic trade shows. Below-the-line marketing like direct mail, sales promotion, sponsorships and exhibitions will grow faster than above-the-line advertising. As teleshopping, telebanking and teleconferencing pick up, we will eventually reach a situation where people can be reached anywhere.

CAN SALESPERSON BE REPLACED?

What happened in the West many years ago is beginning to happen in India too. Salespersons are becoming expensive. And as in the West, companies in India are desperately trying to find answers. Most have not succeeded. At least not yet!

According to the Sales and Marketing Management's annual survey of selling costs in the US, the average cost of a sales call increased more than 11 per cent a year during the last decade, at a time when the average annual sales volume per salesperson rose by only 5.5 per cent. Over the same period, the average number of non-selling hours grew from 12.6 to l5 per week, resulting in an additional 120 non-selling hours per year, and the average cost of training a salesperson jumped 31 per cent from US$ 11,000 to US$ 14,400.

The cost per call is naturally increasing. The average cost of a business-to-business call is now more than US$ 250. The cost per call can vary from a high of US$ 4,300 for industrial machinery to a low of US$ l50 for glass products. But there are companies like IBM and Apple Computers where a sales call can cost over US$ 400 because of the unusual complexity of the product and the selling process.

Another survey by McGraw Hill found that, on an average, 4.6 face-to-face calls are required to close a typical industrial product sale of US$ 1,25,000.

In the US, several changes in the selling environment have contributed to rising selling costs. Some of these are as follows:

1. The emphasis on market segmentation
2. Expensive national account selling
3. Growth in customer service demands

4. Increased transportation costs
5. Greater number of professional buyers
6. Consolidation of distributors who then jointly demand concessions
7. Reduction in the number of vendors approved by customers

A growing number of manufacturers are cutting costs by reaching customers through distributors, other middlemen and direct marketing, rather than through their own sales force. They are using direct mail; applying databased marketing and telemarketing; using faxes as an inexpensive method to reach prospects and customers, and electronic mail from one computer to another since 40 million homes now have personal computers; selling via television either through direct response selling or home-shopping channels (entire channels devoted only to selling products or services); or using the electronic shopping videotex, a two way electronic home-shopping system that links consumers with the seller's computer databanks via cable or telephone lines.

As in the West, companies in India are desperately trying to find answers to rising sales force costs. They have tried vending machines, but this has not been a success as a high incidence of vandalism discourages the use of vending machines. Vandals use fake coins or worse, try to prise the coins out of the machine. Some years ago, vending machines installed at Mumbai's Churchgate station had to be withdrawn. We now witness a strange situation at airports in India, at major cities like Mumbai, Delhi and Chennai, where an attendant is on duty at the vending machine to accept the money and to operate the machine. Thus, the main purpose of saving on manual labour is defeated.

It will be some time before telemarketing can succeed in India. The record of efficiency in India's government-owned telephone industry is poor by international standards. One can spend a lot of time in getting a number or in getting wrong numbers. Your own telephone could occasionally be dead, and repairs await prior gratification of the 'area linesman' who lords it over with his technical power. Telefax depends on the telephone lines and, therefore, telefaxes cannot fare any better. The advent of cell phones has been a saviour, and cell phone marketing has become a preferred clone of telemarketing.

A few direct mail companies have started making some progress. As mass media rates keep increasing and sales force costs keep pace, more direct mail is resorted to. The focus at present has been industrial products, consumer durables and other high-value limited segment markets. There are also alcoholic beverages, which cannot be advertised through mass media and, therefore, rely on direct mail, in-shop promotion and merchandising. With more companies using direct mail, the lists available will become more exhaustive and better classified within the next few years.

The agro-input companies in India have successfully developed an affiliate sales force. These are salespersons who are on the payroll of the distributor, work in villages and small towns, sell a limited range of products, are trained by the parent company and provide a support to the main sales force. This system helps bring down the total field force cost considerably. The cost of every regular salesperson could be equal to the cost of three affiliate salespersons. And the affiliate salespersons will be able to give the commitment and dedication of working in what are termed 'micro-interiors', which the regular salesperson would not be able to do with his urban background and requirements of high levels of 'creature comforts'.

The consumer product companies like those manufacturing cigarettes and soap have also had affiliate salespersons for a long time and, in this case, they have helped ensure more intensive distribution at a lower cost. However, in these industries the affiliate sales force has been geared towards distribution rather than active promotion and distribution.

A pharmaceutical company in Mumbai that had problems for a few years with a militant sales force that wanted more pay for less work embarked on a plan to replace salespersons with direct marketing. They send out mailings on their products and samples by courier. The number of sales managers has been increased, with each given a smaller territory. The sales manager meets the important doctors in the area, though at much longer intervals than the salesperson's visits earlier. The results are said to be good. Although the experiment was started in one region, it has now been expanded to other regions as well, with gratifying results. It is an experiment worth watching. However, if too many others follow the same module, the edge of being different will be substantially blunted and the effectiveness reduced.

India is a long way from the home computer age. Computers are yet too expensive for the average household and computerised shopping will have to wait.

More practical and possible solutions will have to be sought, perhaps like a part-time sales force. Somehow, there is not a single company yet that has made this system work. It is used on a sporadic and seasonal basis by UNICEF, CRY and HelpAge to sell their Christmas cards but that is about all. The legendary Avon sales system and Tupperware network are beginning to be accepted here.

Chief executives and sales managers will have to keep thinking of ways and means of making their salespersons more effective and, at the same time, finding other ways of customer contact, customer promo- tion and customer servicing, which are both effective and economical.

TOWARDS A NEWER MARKETING

Philip Kotler in his book *Kotler on Marketing* says that CEOs are finding that their companies are spending more on marketing and accomplishing less. Kotler says that this happens because they are depending on Neanderthal marketing, which has the following characteristics:

1. Equating marketing with selling
2. Emphasising customer acquisition rather than customer care
3. Trying to make a profit on each transaction rather than profit by managing customer lifetime value
4. Cost-plus pricing rather than target pricing
5. Planning each communication tool separately rather than integrated marketing communication
6. Selling the product rather than trying to understand and meet the customer's real needs

Smart marketing companies are improving their customer knowledge, customer connection technologies and understanding of customer economies. They sometimes invite customers to co-design the product, make flexible market offerings, use a more targeted media and deliver a consistent message through every customer contact.

They use more modern technologies, and are able to identify the more profitable customers and set up different levels of service. Their distribution partners are their partners not adversaries.

Finally, as Kotler says, the premium will go to those companies that invent new ways to create, communicate and deliver value to their target markets. They are marketing visionaries who have market foresight. And the 21st century salesperson is a part of this group.

EIGHT KEYS TO SUCCESS

Bob Kimball, an associate marketing professor at a US college, lists eight keys to success that differentiate a professional salesperson from an average one.

1. *Selling is a skill* that can be learnt through knowledge and expertise about your product and service, your customers and their needs, your competition and your industry.

   Some people we meet seem to be 'born' salespeople. It is heartening for most of us to know that selling is a skill that can be acquired.
2. *You are the most important product.* Professional people accept personal responsibilities for themselves and their lives, committing themselves to personal development and an effectively organised management style. Do you fulfil this?
3. *Relationships, emotions and feelings are the key factors* in sales success. People like to buy from salespeople they like and trust. So treat your customers like VIPs, let them know that their business matters to you, say 'thank you' and mean it, be honest, have a feedback policy and keep communication lines open, and when you make a mistake, acknowledge it.
4. *Identify and develop your prospects.* This would mean a planned way of selecting your prospects, identifying the decision makers, making appointments and using your skills to persuade them to see you personally.

   Also included is providing proper after-sales service and follow-up, so you can build repeat business and referrals. Getting the order is only the beginning of 'creating and retaining' a customer.
5. *A sales call is a performance.* See that everything is organised for it. If it is a presentation in a particular room, check the seating, the microphone, the acoustics, air conditioning, etc. Before each call, check your personal grooming, your bag, visual aids, samples, etc. And during the interview, involve the prospect to make the demonstration a participative one.

6. *Develop effective negotiation skills.* Anyone can make a sale by cutting the price. But to make a sale that is a mutually beneficial package involves negotiating skills.
7. *Objections are your friends.* View them as a means of making your customers express their thoughts and feelings, thereby uncovering their concerns and buying motives. This will help you make the sale.
8. *Always be closing.* If by learning good closing techniques, you think, right from the beginning of the presentation, in terms of building an agreement and helping the prospect decide *how* (not *whether*) to buy, you can complete a mutually beneficial transaction.

TEN KEYS TO POSITIVE HUMAN RELATIONS

To be successful today one needs to know how to get on well with people. Having the highest degree from the most well-known university and being a high ranker may get one a job but it does not ensure success in the job. A person with an average track record at academics may be more successful than the high rankers. It is, therefore, in our own interest to learn how to get on well with people. The following are 10 keys to positive human relations:

1. Speak to people. There is nothing as well received as a cheerful greeting.
2. Smile at people. It takes 72 muscles to frown, only 14 to smile!
3. Call people by name.
4. Be friendly and helpful. (In short, follow the golden rule, 'Do unto others as you would have them do unto you.')
5. Be cordial. Speak and act as if it is a genuine pleasure.
6. Be sincerely interested in people. (Selfish people focus on themselves. Unselfish people focus on others and therein lies the source of their happiness and success.)
7. Be generous with praise and cautious with criticism.
8. Be considerate with the feelings of others.
9. Respect the opinions of others, especially when they differ from yours.
10. Be alert to offer your services. What counts most, off and on the job, is what we do for others.

Index

after-sales service, 119–20
  computers, 119
  consumer durables, 118
  industrial products, 117–18
  insurance business, 118–19
AIDA (Attention, Interest, Desire, Action) formula, 24, 25
Anderson, Rolph, 10
art of active listening, 69–70
art of verbal communication, 66, 67
attending salesperson, 29

body language signals, in sales interview, 100–01
botched follow-up, 113
'boundary-less time zone', 6–7

close, 103
  handling rejection, 104–06
  reasons for inability to close, 104
  war of nerves, 104
  ways of closing, 103
  and women customers, 110–11
communication, non-verbal factors in
  appearance and physique, 65
  body contact/touch, 65
  eye contact, 63–64
  facial expressions, 64
  gestures, 64
  head movements, 64
  posture, 64
  proximity and orientation, 64
  speech, non-verbal aspects, 65
complete customer satisfaction, 121–22
customer
  attention of, 67, 78
  classification, 43–44
  constant contact with, 108–09
  demonstration, 83–85
  expectations, 97–98
  friendship with, 109–10
  needs of, 3–4
  objections from, 90–91
  satisfaction, 120–21
  as star, 62–63
  woman, 110–11

Death of a Salesperson, 13
demonstration, power of, 83–85
direct marketing, by company, 146
Drucker, Peter, 22

empathy, 41, 61, 70, 90

failures of company after success, reasons for, 10–11
friendship trap, 109–10

Hey, I'm the Customer, 121
How to Win Customers, 105
humility and honesty, 127–28

Kimball, Bob, 148
Kotler on Marketing, 147
Kotler, Philip, 10, 41, 143, 147

lead system, 112–13

making of good salespeople, 113–14
MAN (Money, Authority and Need)
  identification, in selling, 44, 45
marketing
  definition of, 4, 5
  in new millennium, 143–44
marketing mix, 5
market research, by salesperson, 52–53
  hints for effective market research, 53–54
Mazur, Paul, 4, 5
McCormack, Mark H., 127
merchandising
  awareness among salespersons for, 116
  design of the package, 116 power of, 114–15
  and retailers, 116–17
  where product is main POP, 117
Miller, Arthur, 13
missionary salespersons, 36–37

Neanderthal marketing, 147
newer marketing approach, 147–48
non-verbal communication. *See* communication, non-verbal factors in

objections, 90–91
  dealing with, 95, 96
  kinds of objections, and possible answers, 93–94
  from women, 110–11
occupation to profession, criteria for, 16–17

paralinguistics, 67
peer pressure, 132–33
personalised selling, 85–86
personal selling, trends in, 10
Petal System, 56
Pie System, 55–56
planning for sale, by salesperson, 39
  bag, with all materials, 46
  categorisation of, customers, 43–44
  daily plan of work, 46
  identification of right person (MAN), 44–45
  territories and customers, selection of, 42–43
  time management principles, 44
  working out call list and journey plan, 46–47
point of purchase (POP) material, 115
presentation, preparation of. *See* sales presentation, training for
Professional Personal Selling, 10
profession, four criteria for, 16–17

sales
  call cost, 57, 144–47
  forecasting system, 54–55
  leads, 111–13
  little things count, 77
  long-term vision, 19–20
  reports, 134–35
salesperson
  and amateur, difference between, 73, 77
  and self-management, 50–51
  and time management, 55–57
  and writing reports, 50–51
  as ambassador of his company, 20–21
  as sales forecaster for his area, 54–55
  companies training, 26, 66
  consumer durables, 31–32
  consumer products, 42
  creating attention, importance of, 78, 81
  criteria for professional salesperson, 15
  customer needs and, 3–4

definition and concept of, 2–3
distractions, controlling of, 81–82
help, by market research, 52
importance of time, 56–57
industrial products, 33–34, 141
initiating contact, different approaches, 82–83
jumping to conclusions, 76–77
maintaining family ties, 126–27
manager of his time, 55–56
as marketing man, 51–52
of pharmaceutical companies, 32
and preconceived impressions, 76
qualities of, 3–4
reasons for failure, 57–58
requirement for
enthusiasm, 27–28
perseverance, 28–29
sincerity, 28
trust and faith, 26
self-confidence and high success attitude, 12–13
structured selling or impromptu speech, 71–72
unwritten code among, 18–19
use of, 'I knew it already,' 62–63
voice, 66–69
vs. traveller, 39, 50
salesmanship, as career, 125–26
salesperson's kit, 21, 46, 66, 77
sales presentation, training for, 75–76
sales report forms
Daily Plan of Work, 137
Field Work Analysis, 139
Monthly Customer Call Analysis, 138
Monthly Review, 140
Monthly Tour Plan, 136
self-esteem, 128, 129–30
selling
challenges in, 9
and complaining customer, 97
different approaches in, 85–88
enthusiasm, sincerity and perseverance (ESP) for, 27–29
ever-changing profession, 13–14
industrial consumables, 33
occupation to profession
criteria for, 16–17
remuneration, 17–18
role of managements, 17
sales associations role, 17
as profession, 14–15
advantages in, 20
four criteria for, 16–17
of semi-consumer products, 32
of service, 35–36
in 21st century
coordinated team efforts, 141–42
role of technology, 142–43, 147
Shapiro, S. Robert, 2
smile, power of, 27–28
Socratic selling, 70–71
speech, 21, 65, 66, 68, 104
strengths, and weaknesses, 131–32
stress prone categories, 133–34
success keys, for professional salesperson, 148–49

target setting method, 55
teamwork, 141–42
telemarketing, 112, 145
The Art of Two Way Communication (film), 77
The Professional (film), 15
tour programme, 55–56
trust building, 124–25

verbatim detailing, 71–72
voice
and AIDA formula, 67
enunciation, 69
importance of, 66
pace, 68–69
pitch, 68
training of, 66–67

What They Don't Teach You at Harvard Business School, 127

About the Author

Walter Vieira founded Marketing Advisory Services Group, Mumbai, India, in 1975 and pioneered Marketing Consulting in India. Prior to that, he spent fourteen years working with various corporations in India—Glaxo, Warner Lambert, and the Boots Company where he was Marketing Head for India, Sri Lanka and Bangladesh.

A Certified Management Consultant (CMC) and later elected a Fellow of the Institute of Management Consultants of India (FIMC) he provided training services and consultancy in business and marketing strategies to several organizations in India and abroad.

Walter Vieira has been Visiting Professor at leading management institutes in India – like Bajaj Institute, Mumbai and ASCI, Hyderabad and has lectured at Business schools—Kellogg, Drexel, Cornell, Rady, URI, Lake Forest, NYU, among others in the USA, Boston Management School, Zaragoza, Spain and other business schools in Thailand, Hong Kong and Nigeria.

He has published more than nine hundred articles in the business and general press, with a column for Business World for over 18 years, and was on the Advisory Board of the Journal of Management Consultants, USA. He presently continues with a fortnightly column in MoneyLife E-magazine entitled *Lessons from the Past.*

Walter Vieira has authored sixteen books, of which three were written jointly with C. Northcote Parkinson and M. K. Rustomji. His first book was *Marketing: Key to Business Success today*. His most recent books are *Marketing in a Digital World* (co-authored with Brian Almeida) and *Customer Value Starvation can kill* (co-authored with Gautam Mahajan).

He has addressed the World Congress of Management Consultants in Rome (1993), Yokohama (1996) and Berlin (1999) and the World Marketing Summit in Dhaka (2012) and Tokyo (2014).

He has been active in social marketing as Advisor for organizations such as Cancer Aid, World Wildlife Fund for Nature and Consumer Education and Research Society (CERS). He is presently Chairman of CERS, India and Trustee for Moneylife Foundation and IDOBRO.

Walter Vieira has served as the President of the Institute of Management Consultants of India (1987-92), was the Founder Chairman of the Asia Pacific Conference of Management Consultants (1989-90), and Chairman of the International Council of Management Consulting Institutes, USA (World apex body) (1997-99).

Walter was awarded the Lifetime Achievement Award for Management Consulting in 2005 by the Indian Management Consulting Institute, and for Marketing in 2009 by INDYS.